SILO is a Four-Letter Word

Leader Language and Group Identity

A Practical Guide to
the New Discipline of Intergroup Leadership

***By* Stanton M Brooks II**

SILO is a Four-Letter Word
Leader Language and Group Identity
A Practical Guide to the New Discipline of Intergroup Leadership

Published by
Active Twist Consulting Group, LLC
https://activetwist.com

First edition | First printing | Paperback edition
ISBN: 979-8-9955224-0-9
Library of Congress Control Number: 2026908424

Editorial and Production Credits
Cover design and illustration by Stanton M. Brooks II
Interior design and typesetting by Stanton M. Brooks II
Editing and proofreading by Jeanne F. Brooks, PhD

Case Study Disclaimer
The case studies presented in this book are illustrative examples derived from the author's professional experience. They are composites and abstractions, and do not represent any single organization, individual, or business situation. Names, structures, timelines, and circumstances have been altered to preserve confidentiality. Any resemblance to actual persons or organizations is coincidental.

Results Disclaimer
This book presents methods, models, and tools intended to support leadership and organizational practice. Results will vary based on context, execution, and external factors. The author and publisher make no guarantees regarding outcomes, performance, or business results arising from the use of this material.

SILO is a Four-Letter Word

Contents

Acknowledgement

This book would not exist without my father and mentor, Stan Brooks, PhD. While we share a name, we have distinct identities.

For more than twenty years of my professional career, he has served as my primary business mentor. He has been a careful listener, a disciplined thinker, and a leader willing to dissect his own career so I could move faster and avoid missteps.

His guidance shaped not only my understanding of organizations, but how I show up with stakeholders and how I lead.

SILO is a Four-Letter Word is more than a synthesis of his academic work. It is a reflection of how he taught me to see people, systems, and responsibility. Whatever clarity you find here traces back to his patience, his rigor, and his example.

Stanton M. Brooks II

Foreword

Intergroup leadership has been a defining thread throughout my professional life, long before I had the language to describe it. My earliest experiences came in the military, where boundary spanning was not an academic concept but a daily necessity. Leading across units, specialties, and identities required a disciplined ability to bridge differences while supporting cohesion.

When I transitioned into the civilian workplace, including roles within several Fortune 500 companies, I was disappointed by how rarely the leaders in these organizations recognized boundary spanning as a discipline, and how often they struggled because of that absence. Despite its importance, intergroup leadership is still invisible in formal education. No university curriculum teaches it, and no established program prepares leaders to master it.

My dissertation was an attempt to address that gap by finding the measurable skills that effective intergroup leaders must develop.

I wanted to move the field beyond theory and toward a practical understanding of what leaders do when they bridge divides. That work laid a foundation, but it was a starting point.

Stanton Brooks II has taken that starting point and carried it into fresh territory. His BRIDGES model is the first structured framework designed to guide leaders through the developmental journey of intergroup leadership. It maps the evolution from leaders who instinctively protect their teams behind walls (guarding boundaries, minimizing exposure, and reinforcing internal identity) to leaders who intentionally weave their teams into the broader ecosystem of the organization.

Through seven distinct bridges, Stanton offers a progression that helps leaders move from isolation to integration, from defensive postures to collaborative engagements, and from group-centric thinking to system-level leadership.

What makes Stanton's contribution so significant is that nothing like this model exists in the current literature. While my research found the skills intergroup leaders must master, Stanton provides the method for developing them. He offers leaders a roadmap for assessing their capabilities, strengthening their competencies, and maturing in their ability to lead across group boundaries. His work fills a void that has long hindered both scholarship and practice.

This book, "SILO is a Four-Letter Word" is clear, practical, and grounded in real-world experience. Stanton weaves storytelling, research, reflection, and application into a framework that leaders can use at once. In a world where intergroup tensions are increasingly visible, and where organizations desperately need leaders who can bridge divides, his contribution is prompt and essential.

I am proud to introduce this work and proud of the scholar who created it. Stanton Brooks II has expanded the field of intergroup leadership in a meaningful way, and I am confident that his BRIDGES model will become a valuable guide for leaders looking to grow beyond the walls that limit them and toward the weaving that strengthens organizations.

Stan Brooks, PhD

Preface

The Bricks We Lay with Words

I have spent over twenty years in rooms full of brilliant people who struggle to help each other. I have watched experts with years of experience sit across the table from each other, and I have felt the energy drop the moment someone says, "That is not our responsibility." I have seen great teams spend months solving the wrong problem because the right information was locked inside another department.

The most capable people in our companies are often the most isolated. This isolation is a Silent Thief. This silent thief steals profit, slows down projects, and wastes the talent we already have.

This is not a book about "collaboration." That word is used so often it has lost its meaning. This is a book about the invisible architecture of trust. It is about how a leader's words and habits determine if a company moves fast or stays stuck.

The Science of the Silo

There is a silence that hurts modern companies. It is the silence that happens when a leader "protects" their team so much that they stop talking to everyone else. We often call these "silos," and they are the biggest cause of project delays and missed goals.

In this book, we look at the research behind why these walls exist. We use the BRIDGES Model to show how to soften those boundaries and build connections that last. This model is built on decades of study, but it is designed to be used on the ground, for real work.

The Vocation of the Bridge Builder

Think of leadership like maintaining a bridge. A bridge does not hold by itself. It requires someone to inspect the cables, clear the deck, and reinforce the joints. If the inspections stop, the cracks widen, and by the time anyone notices, the span is already in trouble. Leadership across teams works the same way. You must constantly maintain the "Story of Us" to keep the walls from going back up.

How to Move Forward

The following pages offer a map. You will see seven levels of leadership maturity, from being Blocked to becoming Seamless. You will find:

- **The High-Performance Scripts:** What to say to lower friction.
- **The Risk Watchlist:** How to spot structural cracks before they compromise progress.
- **The ROI of Connection:** How to turn shared work into a competitive advantage.

Organizations are living systems. The quality of what they build depends on the quality of their connection. The rooms full of people who struggle to help each other can change. The walls are not made of stone; they are built from words and habits. Both can be changed.

The work begins on the next page.

Stanton M Brooks II

Introduction

Executive Overview

The BRIDGES Model for Intergroup Leadership

Intergroup friction caused by a leader's language is a primary drag on organizational speed. The BRIDGES Model provides the architecture to turn isolated silos into a synchronized ecosystem, preventing the Silent Thief from stealing collective intelligence and speed-to-market.

Strategic Concepts

1. ***Biology Creates Silos:*** *Humans are hardwired to categorize people into "The Home Team" (us) and "Another Team" (them). This is not a character flaw; it is an instinct that leadership must actively manage.*
2. ***The Gatekeeper Rule:*** *Every leader controls "Boundary Permeability." Their specific words and habits determine if the gate to their team is locked or open to the rest of the company.*
3. ***Language Precedes Trust:*** *Actions in low-trust environments are not enough. Leaders must use inclusive language to signal safety before cooperation can occur.*
4. ***The Asymmetry of Growth:*** *Early-stage leaders (Levels 1–3) must over-index on communication to overcome the reputation of their silo.*
5. ***Friction is a Tax:*** *Every disconnect between departments presents a "tax" on your business. Reducing this friction is a direct driver of margin.*

Tactical Actions

1. ***Audit the Map****: Assess your current leadership team against the 7 Levels. Identify who is Blocked and who is moving toward Receptive or beyond.*
2. ***Listen for Labels****: Monitor your meetings. Are other departments called by their names, or are they referred to as "They," "Blockers," or "Corporate"?*
3. ***Check the Flow****: Measure how long it takes for a question to travel from one department to another. Slow flow means locked gates.*
4. ***Mandate the "We"****: Stop accepting "My Team" vs. "Your Team" framing in status reports. Demand a "One Company" narrative.*
5. ***Watch for Early Warning Signs****: Accept that regression is normal. Establish a regular review rhythm to catch "us vs. them" habits before they start to harden.*

Exploring the BRIDGES Model

Leadership is usually described as the ability to get people moving toward a single goal. But in large organizations, the hardest part of that job isn't leading a direct team. It is working with the people who do not report to that leader.

The BRIDGES Model is a map for this new kind of leadership. It shows the journey from being a leader who operates behind walls to becoming one who weaves their team into the heart of the company.

To make this journey, it is first necessary to understand why those walls exist in the first place.

The Core Challenge: Us vs. Them

Humans are naturally wired to sort the world into categories. It is an instinct to create a "Home Team" (the people who are trusted and understood) and "Another Team" (the people who are viewed as different or even as a threat).

In the world of science, this is called Social Identity Theory. This research shows that people often feel better about their own group by framing them as "the good guys," while labeling other groups as bureaucrats or as the "blockers."

When a leader acts on these feelings, they are managing Boundary Permeability. This can be thought of as a gate in a wall. A leader's words and actions determine if that gate is locked tight or swinging open to let trust and information flow through it.

The Two Axes of the BRIDGES Model

Moving from a locked gate to a bridge requires focus on two main areas: how a leader talks and what they do.

The Bridge-Building Axis (The X-Axis)

This axis tracks Bridge-Building Behavior. It runs from ISOLATING behaviors (working in a black box) to COLLABORATING behaviors (working in total sync with other teams).

The Leader Language Axis (The Y-Axis)

This axis tracks Leader Language. It runs from EXCLUDES (talk that reinforces walls) to INCLUDES (language that inspires everyone). The goal is to move toward "The Story of Us", or a way of speaking that makes different groups feel like they are part of one shared mission.

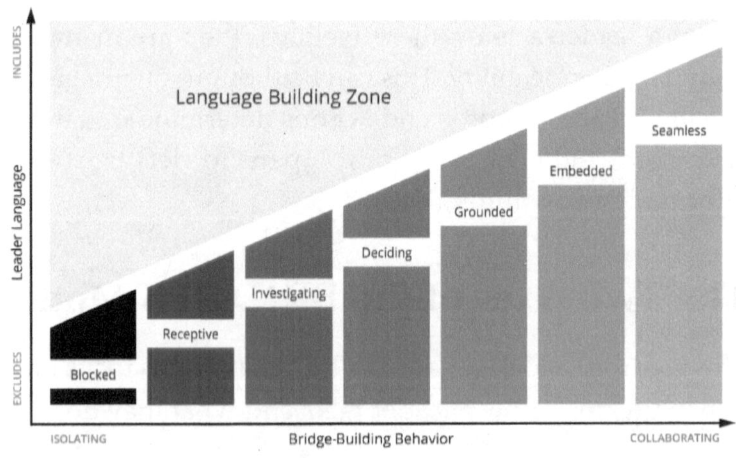

The Complete BRIDGES Model for Intergroup Leadership

The Language Building Zone

In the early stages of leadership, there is often a massive gap between what is said and what is done. In the BRIDGES Model, this is the Language Building Zone. It is shown as a region representing the asymmetry of this gap in communication, and that gap is widest in the early stages of the model.

When trust is low, actions are rarely enough to fix the problem. A leader cannot simply show up to a meeting and expect others to follow. Trust must be built through language first. Inclusive language proves a leader is safe to work with before another team will be willing to open their world to a new partnership.

The Risk of Sliding Back

Building a bridge is difficult, but keeping it standing requires constant effort. In science, the urge to "protect one's own" during times of stress is called In-group Favoritism.

This is why every level in this book includes a Risk Watchlist. These are the early warning signs, and they are small phrases (like "They just don't get it") or small actions (like canceling a joint meeting) that signal a slide backward into isolation.

How to Use This Book

In *SILO Is a Four-Letter Word,* the main chapters explore the seven levels of the **BRIDGES Model**, from **Blocked (Level 1)** to **Seamless (Level 7)**.

These chapters provide:

An Executive Summary covering a high-level view of the concepts covered in the chapter. Each chapter opens with this overview so you can quickly see the strategic concepts and tactical actions at that level. Use it to orient yourself before you dive into the story and the breakdown, or to revisit the big picture when you need to recalibrate.

An example story of a leader facing real friction in their organization. These narratives show how each level plays out in practice and how a Blocked leader operates, how a Receptive leader begins to shift, and so on. The stories make the framework concrete. They do not change in plot or structure; they are the same leaders and situations, framed so you can see the level in action.

A breakdown of the specific language and behaviors that define that level. Here you will find script shifts (what to say instead), language watchlists (phrases to avoid or adopt), and behavioral checklists (concrete actions). This is where you diagnose where you or your team sits and what to change. The breakdown turns the story into tools you can use.

Some guidelines for advancement and some **risks a leader can watch for** to help them hold their ground. Moving up a level is one thing; staying there is another. Regression is normal under stress. Each chapter's Guidelines and Risk Watchlist which are the early warning signs that help you catch "us vs. them" habits before they set in, so you can sustain the progress you have built.

By identifying where a leader stands today, they can begin the deliberate work of building the bridges an organization needs to move faster and win.

Level 1: Blocked (The Isolated Leader)

Executive Summary

The "Blocked" leader operates a "Black Box" department. While they believe they are protecting their team from distraction, they are actually sequestering critical data and stalling decision-making. This isolation creates a "Blind Spot Tax" where the organization makes expensive bets based on incomplete context.

Strategic Concepts

1. ***The Fortress Illusion***: *Leaders often build walls to protect their team's focus, but these walls eventually turn into a prison. The team becomes "operationally excellent but organizationally irrelevant."*
2. ***Silence is Aggression***: *In the absence of communication, other departments do not assume you are busy; they assume you are hostile. A lack of signal may be interpreted as a signal of distrust.*
3. ***Destructive Defense***: *Blocked leaders use language to deflect blame ("It's a planning problem") rather than solve problems. This turns every interaction into a negotiation rather than a collaboration.*
4. ***The Language Gap***: *At this level, the leader lacks the vocabulary to connect. Their "Home Team" dialect creates a barrier that outsiders cannot penetrate.*
5. ***The Dependency Trap***: *When a leader acts as the sole gatekeeper for their department, they become a single point of failure for the entire value chain.*

Tactical Actions

1. ***Kill the Black Box:*** *Institute a mandatory 24-hour acknowledgment rule for all external inquiries. A speedy response builds trust. That speed signals to other teams that the door is open.*
2. ***Humanize the Other Side:*** *Ban the use of the generalized "They" (e.g. , "Sales is annoying"). Force the use of specific names ("David in Sales needs this").*
3. ***Volunteer an Artifact:*** *Do not wait to be asked. Proactively share one draft roadmap or status report with a stakeholder to prove visibility.*
4. ***The "No-Ask" Update:*** *Send a status update to a peer leader without asking for anything in return. Break the transactional cycle.*
5. ***Signal Presence:*** *Physically (or virtually) attend one cross-functional meeting you usually skip, simply to show that the channel is open.*

The Fortress on the Fourth Floor

Background

Diane Kowalski had been leading the Consumer Insights team at Vantage Retail Group for three years. Her department of twelve analysts occupied the northeast corner of the fourth floor. They called it "The Lab."

When Diane first took over, she inherited a beaten-down group. The rest of the company dismissed them as "the spreadsheet people." She decided to protect them.

Under her leadership, The Lab developed its own methods, its own tools, and its own culture. Diane installed a badge reader at the entrance. She claimed it was for data security. She moved their weekly meetings to 7:30 AM, a time she knew no one from other departments would request to attend.

The work was good. Her analysts produced reports that the executive team praised. But somewhere along the way, Diane stopped seeing the other departments as colleagues. She started seeing them as threats.

The Situation

It was early September. Vantage was preparing for its most important quarter. Carlos Ruiz, who led Merchandising, needed updated customer segmentation data to guide their holiday buying decisions. He had sent three emails over two weeks. Each one was more urgent than the last.

Diane had read every one. She just had not responded.

"They want the segmentation model by Friday," her senior analyst mentioned during the Monday stand-up."Carlos is getting vocal about it in the leadership Slack."

Diane crossed her arms."Let him complain. If we cave every time they wave their hands, we will never get our real work done."

Later that week, she gathered her team for a closed-door session. She drew a box on the whiteboard labeled "Consumer Insights." Then she drew arrows pointing into it from all sides. Each arrow was labeled with a different department name.

"See this? Everyone wants a piece of us. None of them appreciate how hard our work is. So here is what we are going to do. We are going dark. We control the information flow. Everything goes through me. If someone from another department reaches out directly, you forward it to my inbox. You do not reply. We protect our process. That is how we protect each other."

The Flashpoint

The situation exploded during the monthly Operations Review. Diane was presenting a new predictive model when the VP asked if Merchandising had seen it.

"We shared some preliminary outputs last quarter," Diane said.

Carlos straightened up."That is not accurate. We have not received any outputs. I have been requesting updated data for weeks without a single response."

The room went quiet.

Diane felt defensive."If they are struggling, that is not a data problem. It is a planning problem."

"It is a data problem," Carlos said."We are making a fourteen million dollar inventory bet based on year-old segments. I have sent emails. I stopped by your office. I had my analysts reach out. What are we supposed to do?"

The VP frowned."This is a cross-functional company, Diane. We succeed or fail together."

"My team does excellent work," Diane said flatly."I will not apologize for protecting them from distraction."

The Cost of the Walls

When the holiday results came in, Merchandising had missed their margin target by nine percent. It was the worst performance in five years.

The post-mortem revealed that several product categories had been over-invested based on outdated customer assumptions. The data that could have prevented this sat unused in The Lab's database.

An external consultant's report described Consumer Insights as "operationally excellent but organizationally isolated." It noted "communication patterns that discourage cross-functional engagement."

When Diane read it, she felt the familiar mix of anger and vindication. They do not understand what it takes to protect quality.

But late that night, alone in The Lab, she allowed herself a different thought.

Maybe the walls I built to protect my team ended up trapping us instead.

She stared at the whiteboard.

The box labeled "Consumer Insights" now looked less like a fortress and more like a prison.

Breaking It Down

The Home Team's Language

At this level, the way a leader speaks is the main cause of friction. Their messages often fail to connect with anyone outside their immediate circle. They may default to "destructive" language that assigns blame or highlights differences instead of building empathy. Without a shared vocabulary, their attempts to share a vision often lead to total misunderstandings. This creates a strong "us versus them" feeling that stops them from seeing any reason to cooperate.

A Blocked leader shows ISOLATING behaviors. They often run their department like a "black box," making decisions or finishing work without talking to the groups that depend on them. While the leader might think they are just moving fast or "protecting" their people, this lack of transparency kills trust. Because another team has no visibility into the process, they start to view the leader with suspicion.

Bridge-Building Behaviors

At Level 1, bridge-building means moving from the ISOLATING end of the Bridge-Building Behavior axis toward COLLABORATING. Right now, the leader's behaviors reinforce the walls instead of creating openings. The work at this level is to recognize what ISOLATING looks like in practice, and to take the first concrete steps that signal the gate is no longer locked.

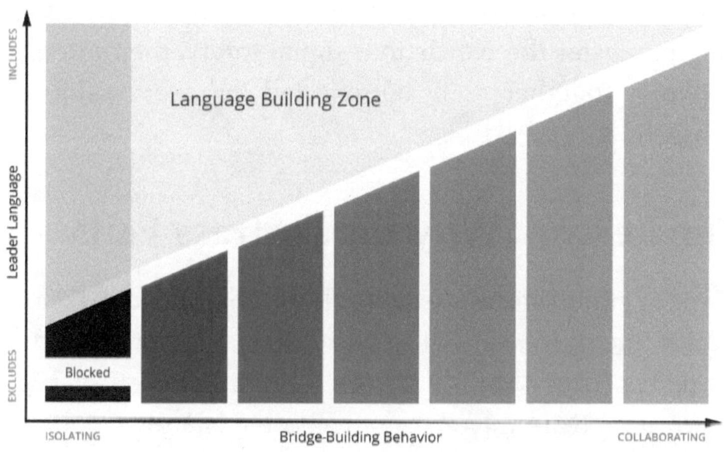

Level 1: Blocked (The Isolated Leader)

The Language Building Zone

Level 1 leaders are deep in the Language Building Zone. There is a massive gap here: the leader has the lowest ability to build bridges, but the highest need to change how they communicate. Because trust is low and silos are strong, a leader cannot simply "act" their way into a partnership yet. The other team isn't ready to play along.

The heavy lifting at this stage must be done through language and this requires talking your way into trust before you can act your way into partnership. Until leaders master the words that signal safety, their attempts to work together will be rejected or seen as just a transaction.

The Lesson: Why the Fortress Fails

Diane's story shows exactly how the "Blocked" level works. She didn't set out to be a villain; she set out to be a protector. But her "Fortress" logic turned a high-performing team into an organizational island.

The Home Team Trap:

Diane defined loyalty as "us against the world." By installing badge readers and 7:30 AM meetings, she signaled to her team that the other team was the enemy of their focus. That framing made every request from Merchandising feel like an intrusion instead of a partnership. The more she protected, the more isolated The Lab became.

The Silent Thief

Because Diane "went dark," the company made a $14 million inventory bet using year-old data. The friction wasn't just a communication issue; it was a performance leak that cost the company a 9% margin miss. The data that could have prevented the over-investment sat unused in The Lab's database, which was a direct result of treating other departments as distractions rather than stakeholders.

The Echo Chamber

In her closed-door sessions, Diane only heard her own team's frustrations. This reinforced the "Blocked" mindset where "they" (the Merchandising team) were seen as a distraction rather than a partner. Without exposure to the cost of her choices, she had no reason to change course until the holiday results made it unavoidable.

The Pivot: Changing the Script

The pivot here is a direct example of how Diane could have used Bridge-Building language to change the reality in the room. During the Operations Review, when Carlos challenged her, Diane defaulted to a "defensive" wall:

"If they are struggling, that is not a data problem. It is a planning problem."

The Script Shift

Using a more strategic filter, Diane should have used Inclusive Language to protect the company's speed-to-market:

"Carlos, I see now that our lack of data is hurting your holiday buying decisions. We have a process gap here that is putting $14 million at risk. I'm moving my team's focus to get you those updated segments by Friday. Let's stay in sync so we don't miss this window."

How Diane Levels Up

To move from Blocked to Receptive, a leader must stop reinforcing the walls. The goal is to move from a defensive stance to one of curiosity.

Listen for this Language

The Generalized "They"

Watch for using "Management" or "Sales" as labels instead of using the specific names of colleagues. When you say "they" or "corporate," you are speaking about a faceless group which makes it easier to dismiss their needs. Naming people (e.g. , "Carlos in Merchandising") turns a category into a person and creates accountability.

The Silent Veto

Staying quiet in a cross-functional meeting only to complain about the decision to your own team later. This behavior signals that you are not truly in the room. Other leaders interpret your silence as disengagement or passive resistance, and they stop expecting you to contribute. The veto happens in the hallway, not in the meeting.

Internal Jargon

Using team-specific acronyms that make outsiders feel like they do not belong in the conversation. Jargon can be efficient within your team, but it excludes others who need to understand. When you notice someone from another department hesitating or asking for clarification, that is a signal to simplify.

The Character Attack

Framing friction as a personality flaw in another team rather than a breakdown in the workflow."They're difficult" or "Carlos doesn't get it" shifts the problem from process to person. That makes collaboration feel impossible because you cannot fix someone else's character. Focusing on the workflow (who needs what, when, and how) keeps the door open.

The "Not Our Job" Reflex

Using words that reinforce a strict divide, such as "That's their problem" or "We don't do that here." These phrases draw a hard line between your team and others. Once that line is spoken, it is hard to cross. Reframing around shared outcomes ("If we don't fix this, we both miss the target") invites partnership instead of blame.

Behaviors to Observe

The 24-Hour Acknowledgment

Ensure every external inquiry gets a response within one business day to kill the "black box" reputation. You do not have to solve the request in 24 hours, but you should acknowledge it. A simple "I received this; I'll have an update by [date]" signals that the gate is not locked. It is the first behavior that builds trust before you deliver.

The Artifact Handshake

Proactively send a draft roadmap or status report to a stakeholder before they have to ask for it. This flips the dynamic from "they are pulling on us" to "we are offering visibility." One shared document can reduce dozens of status emails and show that you see the other team as a partner, not an interruption.

The Visibility Signal

Attend the cross-functional town hall or update meeting you usually skip, simply to show you are present. Your presence communicates that you are actively in the room. You do not have to speak; showing up signals that the channel is open. It is a low-effort, high-signal behavior at Level 1.

The "No-Ask" Update

Reach out to a peer leader to share a win or a change without asking for a single thing in return. Most cross-functional communication is transactional ("I need X from you"). A no-ask update breaks that pattern. It says: "I am keeping you in the loop because we are on the same team." That builds goodwill for the next time you do need something.

The Constraint Check

Ask a peer leader, "What is your biggest blocker right now?" to signal you see them as a partner. The question alone shifts the frame from "my priorities" to "our constraints." It invites them to name what is in the way, and it opens the door for you to help or at least to understand. That is how bridge-building starts.

Level 2: Receptive (The Aware Leader)

Executive Summary

The "Receptive" leader creates a dangerous illusion of alignment. They attend the meetings and smile in the hallways, creating a "Politeness Tax" where the organization believes collaboration is happening, but work is still being executed in silos. This stage is often where speed dies quietly. It does not die from conflict, but from passive non-participation.

Strategic Concepts

1. ***The "Guest" Mentality:*** *At this level, leaders treat cross-functional meetings as events they are "visiting" rather than work they co-own. They are present in the room but absent from the outcome.*
2. ***Awareness ≠ Action:*** *Recognizing that a silo exists is not the same as breaking it down. Many leaders get stuck here, mistaking their good intent ("I want to help") for impact.*
3. ***The Bandwidth Defense:*** *"Receptive" leaders often use "resource constraints" as a polite way to shut the door; to decline partnership without seeming hostile.*
4. ***Inconsistent Signaling:*** *Trust is stalled because the leader sends mixed messages and uses inclusive language in public meetings but reverts to "us vs. them" complaints in private.*
5. ***Fragile Momentum:*** *The door is cracked open, but the habit of partnership is weak. One bad interaction or stressful deadline will cause the leader to retreat to Level 1.*

Tactical Actions

1. ***The Discovery Session**: Schedule a 30-minute meeting with a peer solely to learn their goals. The agenda is forbidden to include specific "asks" or deliverables.*
2. ***The Workflow Shadow**: Do not just read the report; sit in on the partner team's internal review to see the friction they face firsthand.*
3. ***Explain the "Why"**: When saying no or delaying a request, explicitly explain the constraints. Turn a rejection into a transparency moment.*
4. ***The Joint Artifact**: Move beyond talk. Draft a simple one-page problem statement and ask a leader from the other team to edit it. Co-creation forces connection.*
5. ***The 48-Hour Loop**: If an issue is "parked" in a meeting, mandate a follow-up response within two days. Silence after a meeting is a trust-killer.*

The Door Left Ajar

Background

Six months ago, Nathan Okafor would not have been caught dead at a Marketing meeting. As the Director of Data Engineering at Bellwether Financial Services, he had spent four years cultivating what he called a "clean separation of concerns." His team of fourteen engineers built and maintained the data infrastructure that powered everything from fraud detection to customer analytics. They were the backbone of the company. And backbones did not need to attend brainstorming sessions about brand positioning.

Then came a comment from the CTO during a routine quarterly review.

"Nathan, your team does incredible work. But I keep hearing that other departments feel like they are shouting into a void when they need something from Data Engineering. What is going on over there?"

Nathan bristled. His team delivered. They hit their SLAs. They maintained 99. 97% uptime. What more did these people want?

Then he made the mistake of actually asking. A quiet conversation with a peer revealed that "working with Data Engineering" had become shorthand for "do not bother trying."

His team was seen as technically brilliant but impossible to reach. A locked room that occasionally slid deliverables under the door.

The feedback stung. For the first time in years, Nathan wondered if the walls he had built were not protecting his team so much as imprisoning them.

The First Steps

It began with small changes. Nathan added himself to the Marketing team's newsletter distribution list. He accepted a calendar invite to the Customer Experience committee meeting. He had declined it so many times that people had stopped inviting him. He walked over to the Sales floor and introduced himself to the new VP.

"I have heard a lot about your team," she said."Honestly, I was not sure you existed. I thought Data Engineering was just an email address that sometimes replied."

Nathan laughed, though it came out forced."We exist. We are just usually heads-down. But I am trying to be more available."

A door had been opened. Just a crack, but it was open.

The Promise

Two weeks later, Nathan attended his first Marketing leadership meeting. Near the end, the CMO raised a challenge. They could not get reliable attribution data for digital campaigns. It was hard to prove ROI to the board.

A junior marketing manager named Derek spoke up hesitantly."I have sent a few tickets to Data Engineering, but I have not heard back."

All eyes drifted to Nathan.

"I was not aware of that," he said."I am sorry the tickets fell through the cracks. Send me the details and I will make sure it gets attention. We want to help."

The meeting ended positively. But as Nathan walked back to his floor, he felt uneasy. We want to help. He had meant it. But did his team have bandwidth? Would they see this as a priority?

The Flashpoint

The attribution issue turned out to be tangled up with legacy systems, inconsistent tracking codes, and a third-party vendor whose documentation was essentially fictional. A week later, Nathan's lead team was tense.

"I told you this would happen," his lead engineer said."We opened the door to Marketing, and now they are camping out in our living room. Every day it is another quick question that takes three hours. We are not a service desk."

Nathan felt the old instincts kicking in. The urge to protect his team. To push back against external demands. The stress of the past week, the pressure from above, the complaints from his own people. And in that moment, the carefully measured language he had been practicing gave way to something older.

"You know what? You are right. Marketing does not understand what they are asking for. They think data just appears because they want it. They have no idea how much work goes into making these systems run."

He caught himself. But not before the words had landed. His engineers exchanged a look. The kind that said there is the Nathan we know.

"Sorry," Nathan said."I should not have said it like that. Venting about Marketing is not going to fix anything."

But the damage lingered. In one unguarded moment, he had slipped back into the old patterns.

The Accounting

By the end of the month, the attribution project had been officially "deprioritized." Nathan sent an apologetic email explaining that resource constraints made it impossible to deliver.

The CMO's reply was cordial but cool: Thanks for the update. We will explore some workarounds on our end. I appreciate you attending the meeting a few weeks ago. Hopefully we can find more opportunities to collaborate down the road.

Nathan stared at the email."Hopefully we can find more opportunities." It was the kind of polite language people used when they had given up on you.

That night, Nathan sat in his home office. He pulled up the Marketing newsletter he had subscribed to six weeks ago. He had not read any of them. They had piled up in a folder labeled "Cross-Functional Stuff."

I wanted this to be different, he thought. I saw the problem. I tried to fix it.

But trying was not the same as doing. Attending a meeting was not the same as building a relationship. Saying "we want to help" was not the same as actually helping.

He was starting to understand something important. Awareness was not the same as action. Good intentions, without consistency, were just another kind of silence.

The Morning After

The next day, Nathan did something small. He forwarded one of the unread newsletters to his team with the following subject line:

"Worth skimming. Helps to know what other parts of the company are working on."

He kept the newsletter subscription active. He kept the Customer Experience meeting on his calendar. And when Derek sent a follow-up message a few weeks later, tentative and clearly expecting to be ignored, Nathan replied within the hour.

Hey Derek. Sorry again about how the last project went. I would like to understand your team's analytics needs better. Could we grab 30 minutes next week? I am not promising miracles, but I want to make sure we are on the same page.

Derek's response came back immediately:

"That would be great. Thanks for reaching out. I know your team is busy. I really appreciate it."

It was a small thing. Just a meeting. No guarantees, but the door, at least, was open again.

Breaking It Down

The Home Team's Language

At this stage, the leader knows that language matters. They make their first real efforts to use "constructive" words to build understanding. However, these efforts are often inconsistent. A receptive leader might speak well in a scheduled meeting but slip back into "us vs. them" habits when they are stressed or talking casually with their own team. Their words signal a good intent, but they lack the consistency needed to build deep trust with other teams.

Bridge-Building Behaviors

Behaviors at this level shift from ISOLATING toward COLLABORATING. The leader starts to show up in spaces they used to avoid. These steps are new and are not yet part of the leader's daily routine. A Receptive leader might attend a cross-functional meeting or ask about a neighbor's roadmap, but they rarely follow through with deep coordination. The "black box" is slightly open, but the walls are still standing.

The Language Building Zone

At Level 2, the leader is still in a high-intensity part of the Language Building Zone. The shift is mostly internal, and it is an acknowledgment that a problem exists. The asymmetry is still a major hurdle: the leader's actions are still too weak to carry the relationship. They cannot "act" their way into partnership because trust has not been earned yet. The burden remains on their language to align their intent with their impact. If they fail to speak clearly here, their small steps will be misunderstood, and they risk sliding back to Blocked.

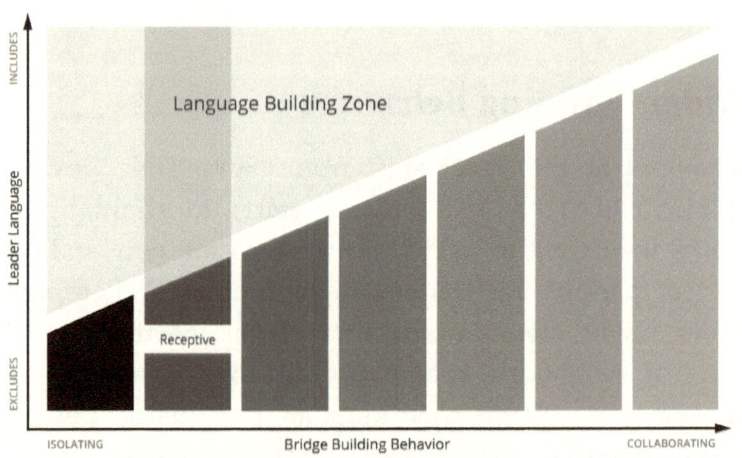

Level 2: Receptive (The Aware Leader)

The Lesson:
The Danger of the Cracked Door

Nathan's story shows that awareness is not the same as action. He opened the door, but didn't walk through it.

The Home Team Trap: When Nathan's lead engineer complained about Marketing "camping out in the living room," Nathan's old instincts took over. He agreed that "they" didn't understand the work, which reinforced the wall he had just tried to crack. That moment of agreement with his team, when he was venting instead of reframing, undid the goodwill he had built by showing up at the Marketing meeting. The crack in the door closed just a little more.

The Silent Thief: By "deprioritizing" the attribution project through an apologetic email, Nathan allowed the thief of friction to steal the company's ROI. The project failed not because of a lack of skill, but because of a lack of consistent connection. The polite "resource constraints" explanation felt like transparency to Nathan, but to Marketing it felt like a door sliding shut. The company lost more than a project; it lost trust in the bridge Nathan had started to build.

The Echo Chamber: Nathan subscribed to the newsletter but never read it. He attended the meeting but didn't build the relationship. This is the "Aware" trap: thinking that being in the room is the same as being in the partnership. Presence without follow-through signals interest but not commitment. Other teams learn to stop expecting real collaboration, and the Receptive leader stays stuck between Blocked and Investigating.

The Pivot: Changing the Script

The pivot here shows how Nathan could have used Bridge-Building language to hold the ground he had gained. When his engineers complained, Nathan defaulted to language that EXCLUDES:

"Marketing doesn't understand what they're asking for. They think data just appears because they want it."

The Script Shift

To protect the company's Collective Intelligence, Nathan should have used The Story of Us to leverage language that moves toward INCLUDES and reframes the struggle:

"Team, I hear the frustration. Marketing is under pressure to prove ROI to the board, and they need our expertise to do it. It feels like they are camping in our living room because we haven't built a shared workspace yet.

Let's look at the tracking codes together and show them what a realistic timeline looks like so we can solve this for the company."

Reviewing the Receptive Level

A leader at the Receptive level is aware of the friction but lacks the habits to fix it. These are observable "leaks" in performance:

The Polite Silo

Attending meetings but remaining a "guest" who does not offer deep coordination. You are in the room, but you are not co-owning the outcome. Other leaders notice the difference between someone who shows up and someone who leans in. Without co-ownership, the door stays cracked but the relationship never deepens.

The Bandwidth Wall

Using "resource constraints" as a polite way to shut the door when things get difficult. The phrase sounds reasonable, but at Level 2 it often masks a retreat. When you say "we don't have bandwidth" without explaining the trade-offs or offering a path forward, the other team hears "we are not prioritizing you." Transparency about constraints builds trust; using them as a blanket "no" doesn't.

Inconsistent Intent

Using inclusive words in public but reverting to "us vs. them" narratives in private. In the meeting you say "we want to help"; in the hallway with your team you say "they don't get it." That inconsistency is visible over time. People notice when your private language doesn't match your public language and that's when trust begins to stall.

The Passive Calendar

Accepting invites to attend cross-functional sessions but failing to prepare or follow up on the items discussed. Showing up unprepared signals that the meeting is a checkbox, not a commitment. Failing to follow up on parked items signals that the conversation didn't matter. Both erode the trust you are trying to build at Level 2.

How Nathan Levels Up

To move to the Investigating level, Nathan must move from passive awareness to active curiosity. He must walk through the door he opened.

Listen for this Language

The "Why" Inquiry

Ask "Why is this impact happening now?" instead of just "What do you need?" to find the root cause. The "What" question gets you a request; the "Why" question gets you the context you need.

When you understand the pressure the other team is under you can align your response with their reality instead of simply reacting to their ask.

Specific Validation

Instead of saying "I hear you," say "I can see how this delay is affecting your specific lead time." Generic acknowledgment feels like politeness; specific validation shows you have paid attention. Naming the actual impact, such as the lead time, the launch date, or the customer, signals that you see them as a partner with real constraints, not a category.

Vocabulary Adoption

Intentionally use one technical term from another team's domain correctly in a meeting. This is a small but visible signal that you have done the homework. It shows you are not just visiting their world; you are learning its language. One term, used correctly, can shift the dynamic from "guest" to "collaborator."

The Constraint Frame

Replace "We can't" with "Here is the resource reality we are managing." "We can't" shuts the door; the constraint frame opens a conversation. When you explain the trade-offs, such as what you would have to deprioritize, what timeline is realistic, you give the other team information they can work with. They can adjust expectations, escalate, or propose a compromise. Silence or a flat no leaves them in the dark.

The Clarity Check

Ask a peer, "Did my explanation make sense to your team, or was it too technical?" This question does two things: it signals that you care about their experience, and it surfaces miscommunication before it becomes friction. At Level 2, your explanations may still default to your team's dialect. The clarity check is a habit that pulls you toward a shared vocabulary.

Behaviors to Observe

The Discovery Session

Schedule a 30-minute meeting with a peer solely to learn about their goals, with no other agenda. No asks, no deliverables, no status updates, just a focus on your team's current goals. This behavior forces you out of the transactional pattern. It builds the context that makes future collaboration possible and signals that you see them as a partner, not a stakeholder to manage.

The Workflow Shadow:

Ask to sit in on another team's internal review to see their daily friction firsthand. Reading a report is not the same as watching how decisions get made, where bottlenecks appear, and how language shapes outcomes. One shadow session can replace months of assumptions with a single dose of reality. This simple act also signals that you are willing to step into their world.

The Reasoning Share

When sharing a decision, explicitly explain the "Why" and the constraints behind it. At Level 2, the other team has low trust in your follow-through. When you say no or delay a request, they may assume the worst unless you give them the reasoning. "Here is why we are deprioritizing this" turns a rejection into a transparency moment and keeps the door of communication open.

The Joint Artifact

Draft a simple one-page problem statement and ask a leader from the other team to edit it with you. Co-creation forces connection. The act of editing together, not just reviewing, builds shared ownership. You are no longer handing something over the wall; you are building something on the bridge.

The Parking Lot Follow-up

Take an issue that was sidelined in a meeting and reach out to address it within 48 hours. Silence after a meeting is a trust-killer. When something gets "parked," the other team doesn't know if it was forgotten or ignored. A short follow-up: "Here is where we landed on the parking lot item" signals that you are accountable and that the conversation mattered.

How to Avoid Sliding Back

The greatest risk at this level is the urge to retreat when the initial work of connection feels awkward or slow.

Language Risks

The "Us vs. Them" Relapse

Catching yourself saying "They just don't get it" after a hard meeting. That phrase is a regression signal. It flattens the other team into a category and excuses you from the important work of understanding. When you hear yourself say it, pause: What specifically don't they get? What have you done to help them get it? The relapse is normal under stress; the recovery is choosing different words next time.

The Polite Dismissal

Using phrases like "We'll take that under advisement" as a code for "We are going to ignore this." Polite language that carries no commitment erodes trust faster than a direct no. If you cannot do something, say so and explain why. If you need time to decide, say when you will follow up. "Under advisement" without a timeline is a soft version of closing a door.

The Fake Yes

Saying "We want to help" when there is no intention or capacity to do the work. This is the Receptive leader's signature leak. The words sound inclusive, but without follow-through they teach the other team that your yes is meaningless. One fake yes does more damage than a clear no with an explanation.

The Technical Shield

Retreating into complex jargon to shut down a conversation with a non-technical peer. When the conversation gets uncomfortable, it is tempting to hide behind your team's vocabulary. The other person may nod and disengage, which means you have just closed the door with politeness. If you cannot explain it simply, offer to schedule a deeper dive; do not use jargon as a veto.

The Silent Veto

Staying silent in a joint meeting when you disagree, only to voice opposition to the Home Team later. Your silence in the room reads as agreement or disengagement; your opposition in the hallway reads as bad faith. The other team will eventually hear that you said one thing with them and another behind closed doors. Trust requires saying the hard thing in the room, or at least naming that you need to think about it and will come back.

Behavioral Risks

The "One-and-Done" Trap

Attending a meeting once, feeling awkward, and never returning. The first cross-functional meeting at Level 2 is often uncomfortable. You may not know the norms, the inside references, or the unspoken expectations. The trap is treating that discomfort as a signal to retreat. Consistency and showing up again is what turns "guest" into "participant."

The Ghosting Pattern

Letting a difficult email thread with a peer go unanswered for more than two days. At Level 2, response time is a trust signal. When the thread is hard, whether it is a disagreement, a delayed deliverable, an awkward ask, the urge to avoid it is strong. But silence is read as hostility or indifference. A short "I need to think about this; I'll respond by [date]" is better than no response at all.

The Bunker Instinct

Canceling cross-functional syncs the moment the Home Team is under pressure to "focus on real work." This instinct treats internal work as real and cross-functional work as optional. The message to the other team is clear: when the going gets tough, you disappear. Protecting the bridge under stress is what separates Receptive from Blocked; canceling a cross-functional sync is a slide back.

The Proxy War

Sending a junior staff member to deliver bad news to a peer leader instead of doing it yourself. Bad news is part of partnership. When you delegate the hard conversation, you signal that the relationship is not important enough for you to show up. The peer leader will remember who showed up and who did not. Own the message; it builds trust even when the message is no.

The Active Avoidance

Declining invites from other departments without suggesting a better time to connect. A simple "I can't make this one" is a closed door."I can't make this one; can we do Thursday afternoon or a 15-minute sync this week?" keeps the door open. The alternative you propose signals that the connection matters to you.

Level 3: Investigating (The Open Leader)

Executive Summary

The "Investigating" leader acts as an organizational cartographer, mapping the actual terrain of partner teams. This eliminates the "Re-Work Tax." This hidden tax is the capital wasted building products or processes that fail upon launch because they were designed in a vacuum.

Strategic Concepts

1. ***The Map is Not the Territory***: *Org charts do not show how work actually happens. Leaders must actively investigate the informal networks, pressures, and constraints that drive partner teams.*
2. ***The Audit Paradox***: *Sudden questions after years of silence trigger suspicion, not gratitude. Another team will assume it is an audit unless it is framed as help.*
3. ***Extraction vs. Exchange***: *Investigating fails if it is purely extractive ("Give me your data"). It succeeds only when it is reciprocal ("Here is how your data helped us").*
4. ***Language Alignment***: *Leaders must stop forcing their jargon on others and start adopting the vocabulary of the ecosystem. Speaking the partner's dialect is the fastest way to build credibility.*
5. ***Fragile Authority***: *The leader is entering territory where they have no positional authority. Influence here is generated solely by curiosity and the ability to listen without defending.*

Tactical Actions

1. ***Preface with Value:*** *Never ask for data without first stating the problem you are solving for them. (e.g. , "To help you hit your Q4 target, I need to understand X.")*
2. ***Publish the Loop:*** *Do not just gather feedback; report on it. Send a "You Said, We Did" summary that links another team's input to specific changes in your plan.*
3. ***Adopt Their Metrics:*** *Include at least one KPI from a partner team (e.g. , "Support Ticket Volume") in your own internal monthly business review.*
4. ***The "Messy" Invite:*** *Stop waiting for perfection. Invite a partner stakeholder to edit the "ugly draft" to prove you want co-creation, not just sign-off.*
5. ***The Glossary Check:*** *In mixed meetings, pause to define acronyms. If a term isn't understood by everyone in the room, do not use it.*

The Cartographer

Background

Samira Okonkwo had been asking questions for three months straight. As the Vice President of Product Development at Meridian Software, she had spent her first two years focused inward. Building her team. Shipping features. Hitting deadlines. But a botched product launch last fall had forced her to confront an uncomfortable truth. Her team was building in isolation, and it was costing the company.

The launch failure had not been a technical problem. The code was solid, the features were elegant, and her engineers had delivered on time. The problem was that nobody in Sales knew how to position the product. Customer Support had not been trained on the new workflows. Marketing had created campaigns based on assumptions that turned out to be wildly wrong. Her team had built what they thought was right, announced it, and expected everyone else to catch up.

That was not going to work anymore.

So Samira embarked on what she privately called her "cartography project." An attempt to map the terrain of the departments she had been ignoring for years. She wanted to understand how Sales actually sold, how Support actually supported, how Marketing actually marketed. She wanted to learn their language, their pressures, their constraints. It was much harder than she had expected.

The Discovery Sessions

Samira started with informal meetings with leaders from other departments. Her first session was with Roland, the Director of Sales Enablement, who had a reputation for being territorial.

She came prepared with questions, not answers.

"I am trying to understand something," Samira said."When we release a new feature, what happens on your end? Walk me through it like I have never seen it before."

Roland looked surprised. In his experience, Product leaders showed up to tell him things, not ask.

What followed was a forty-five minute education. Roland explained how his team scrambled to create sales decks from incomplete documentation. How they often learned about features at the same time as customers. How they had developed workarounds to compensate for what he called "the information vacuum."

"The worst part," Roland said, "is that when a deal falls through because we did not know about some limitation, Sales takes the hit. Not Product. We are the ones explaining to the VP why we lost a two hundred thousand dollar contract because of something we did not even know existed."

Samira took notes furiously."That is not okay. I had no idea it was this bad."

"Can I ask you something else? If you could design the ideal handoff from Product to Sales, what would it look like for you and your team?"

Roland paused. No one from Product had ever asked him that question.

The Language Experiments

In the weeks that followed, Samira continued her discovery sessions across the organization. Each conversation revealed something new. A pain point she had never considered. A process she had never understood. A piece of jargon that meant something completely different depending on who was saying it.

In Product Development, "ship" meant pushing code to production. In Marketing, it meant launching a campaign. In Sales, it meant closing a deal. Same word, three different meanings. No wonder their communication broke down.

Samira began experimenting with her own vocabulary. In meetings with Sales, she talked about "customer value" instead of "feature sets." With Marketing, she asked about "positioning" instead of diving into the technical specifications.

The results were mixed. Some reframes landed perfectly. Others obscured rather than clarified. Speaking another team's language was not just about using different words. It was about understanding what those words meant to each of them.

The Flashpoint

A few weeks later, Samira found herself in an uncomfortable meeting with Roland.

"I have to be honest with you," Roland said. His tone was cooler than before."My team is starting to feel like you are using us."

"Using you how?"

"You have been sitting in on our training sessions, reading our internal wikis, asking my reps about their objections. At first it seemed helpful. But now it feels like you are gathering intelligence. Like you are building a case against us."

Samira felt a flash of frustration. She had been so careful to explain her intentions. And still it was not enough.

"Roland, everything I have learned from your team, I have used to advocate for changes in Product that make your lives easier. I pushed to move the Q2 integration up specifically because you told me about the upcoming renewal window."

"I know. And I appreciate it. But my reps do not see that. They see a VP from another department poking around their work. Right now, information flows out from my team, but nothing flows back. It feels extractive."

Samira sat with that. She had been a diligent investigator. But she had not been a communicator. She had been gathering insights without showing what she was doing with them.

"What would help?"

"Close the loop. When you learn something from us and act on it, tell us. Show us the connection between what we shared and what changed."

"I can fix that," she said."From now on, every time I make a decision influenced by something I learned from Sales, I will make that connection explicit."

The New Rhythm

Over the following months, Samira developed a new rhythm. Discovery sessions continued. But now she supplemented them with "feedback loops." Regular updates showing how input from other teams had shaped Product decisions.

She created shared documents titled "What Sales Taught Us" and "What Support Taught Us." Each document was populated with specific examples. Timeline adjustments. Documentation changes. Training videos revised based on feedback. Each document was visible to everyone in the company. A public record of how cross-departmental learning was influencing Product Development.

The tone shifted. People who had been wary of her questions started volunteering information unprompted. Marketing sent early campaign drafts. Support started flagging potential issues before they escalated.

It was not seamless. There were still moments of friction, still misunderstandings that required careful navigation. But the momentum was real. The walls between Product and the rest of the company were starting to show cracks.

The map was not finished yet. There were still territories to explore, still languages to learn, still trust to build. But Samira no longer felt like she was operating in the dark.

She was starting to see the whole landscape. And slowly finding her place within it.

Breaking It Down

Leaders at the Investigating level act as the "Open" archetype. They have moved beyond just knowing the silo exists; they are now actively trying to understand the reality of another team. They spend their time mapping the territory, asking questions, and learning the pressures that other groups face. While their momentum is positive, they still hit bumps where their intent does not quite match their impact.

The Home Team's Language

At this stage, the leader focuses on refining their speech to bridge the gap between groups. They are moving away from "us vs. them" talk and trying to use words that resonate with another team. This is a time of experiments.

The leader is asking better questions and trying to speak the "language" of others to build trust. However, they still lack perfect nuance, and some of their messages may still miss the mark.

Bridge-Building Behaviors

Behaviors at this level shift from ISOLATING toward COLLABORATING. The leader is explicitly "reaching across the aisle" to start real collaboration. They might start joint reviews or invite people from another team to join early planning sessions. There is clear progress toward an open environment, but a fully shared workflow is not yet real.

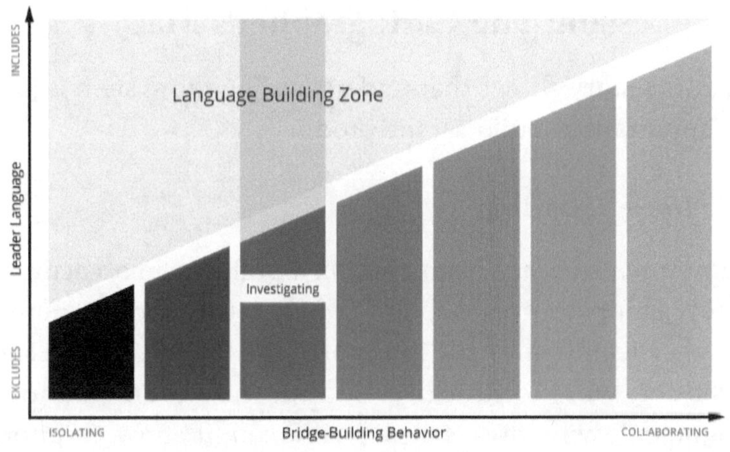

Level 3: Investigating (The Open Leader)

The Language Building Zone

Level 3 is a critical phase in the Language Building Zone. While the leader is taking action, those actions are still fragile. Because the leader is entering new territory, their questions can be easily misunderstood as an "audit" or a "power grab." The asymmetry remains: the leader's language must work harder than their actions. They must use clear words to explain why they are asking questions so that another team does not feel attacked or spied on.

The Lesson: The Cartographer's Map

Samira's story shows that understanding the system is just as important as building the product.

The Home Team Trap

Samira realized her team had been building in a vacuum. They shipped great code, but because they ignored another team (Sales and Support), the launch failed. The product was technically sound; however, without alignment with how Sales positioned it, how Support trained on it, or how Marketing campaigned for it, the launch became a case study in siloed execution. The trap is assuming that "shipping" means the work is done when another team's reality has never been mapped.

The Silent Thief

The lack of shared language meant "ship" meant something different to everyone. This confusion is a thief of Speed-to-Market. In Product, "ship" was code to production; in Marketing, a campaign launch; in Sales, closing a deal. When the same word carries different meanings, handoffs break down and rework multiplies. The thief is invisible until the launch fails, and by then the cost is already paid.

The Echo Chamber

Even when Samira tried to help, people were suspicious of her motives. They saw her "discovery" as an "intelligence gathering" mission. This is the risk of investigating without "closing the loop." When you ask questions but never show what you did with the answers, the other team has no way to know whether you are learning or auditing. Closing the loop and making the connection between their input and your decisions visible turns investigation into partnership.

The Pivot: Changing the Script

The pivot here shows how Samira used Bridge-Building language to prove she was there to help, not to take over. When people felt she was being extractive, she changed how she spoke.

The Script Shift

To protect the company's Collective Intelligence, Samira stopped just asking questions and started showing the value of the answers:

"Roland, I'm creating a 'What Sales Taught Us' document for my engineers. I want to show them exactly how the $200K deal fell through so we can fix the documentation. I'm not here to audit your reps; I'm here to make sure our next roadmap solves the problems your team is seeing in the field."

Reviewing the Investigating Level

A leader at the Investigating level is active but often misinterpreted. Look for these performance "leaks":

The Audit Trap

Asking questions that sound like an interrogation rather than an investigation. The difference is intent and framing. An investigation is framed as "I want to understand so we can improve"; an interrogation feels like "I am checking up on you." When your questions are not preceded by context or followed by visible use of the answers, the other team will assume the worst. Frame your intent explicitly and close the loop so they see the connection.

Extractive Learning

Gathering insights from another team but never showing them how that info changed your plans. At Level 3, you are asking for a lot: their time, their perspective, and their constraints. If they never see their input reflected in your decisions or documentation, they will stop giving it. The "You Said, We Did" summary is not optional at this level; it is the proof that learning is reciprocal.

Analogical Blindness

Using metaphors that make sense to the Home Team but confuse or alarm everyone else. Your team's shorthand: "ship," "pipeline," and "blocker" may mean something different or sound hostile to another department. When you use a metaphor in a mixed meeting, pause to check if it landed. If someone looks confused or defensive, clarify or choose different words.

Fragile Momentum

Reaching across the aisle but retreating the moment another team shows suspicion or pushback. At Level 3, you will encounter resistance. Someone may say "this feels like an audit" or "why do you need this?" The fragile response is to withdraw. The Investigating response is to name the concern, explain your intent, and offer to close the loop so they can see the value of the exchange.

How Samira Levels Up

To move to the Deciding level, Samira must move from "trying" to "committing," and she needs to choose to make the partnership permanent.

Listen for this Language

Preface with Value

Before asking for data, state the specific problem you are solving for them."I need your input on X so we can fix the handoff that cost the $200K deal" is very different from "Can you send me your process doc?" The preface signals that you are not auditing; you are solving a shared problem. It gives them a reason to invest in the conversation.

The "Echo" Technique

Paraphrase a counterpart's concern to prove you understand it before you offer a solution."So what I'm hearing is that your team learns about features at the same time as customers. Is that right?" This does two things: it shows you are listening, and it gives them a chance to correct you. Misunderstanding is common at Level 3; the echo reduces it before you act.

Adopt Their Metrics

Use an outcome metric that another team values (like "tickets reduced") in your own reports. When you speak in their KPIs, you signal that you see their world. Including one of their metrics in your monthly review is a visible commitment that their success is part of your dashboard, not just your team's.

The "We" Reframe

Replace "My Team" and "Your Team" with "We" when talking about a shared blocker."We're blocked on the handoff" is different from "Your team isn't giving us what we need." The "We" reframe shifts the frame from blame to shared problem-solving. It is a small linguistic change with a large impact on how the conversation lands.

Glossary Alignment

Use a technical term from another team's world correctly to show you are learning their language. One term, used in context, signals that you have done the homework. It builds credibility faster than a dozen generic questions. Pay attention to the words they use and adopt them when you speak about their domain.

Behaviors to Observe

Publish the Loop

Send a "You Said, We Did" summary that lists what you changed based on their feedback. This behavior turns investigation into exchange. When the other team sees their input reflected in your decisions, such as updated documentation, adjusted timelines, and revised training, they stop seeing you as an auditor and start seeing you as a partner. Publish the loop regularly, not once.

Draft-Stage Inclusion

Invite another team to a "messy" working session instead of just the final review. When you only show up with a polished deliverable, you are asking for sign-off, not collaboration. Inviting them into the messy draft signals that you want their input when it can still shape the outcome. It is a high-trust behavior that accelerates Level 3 momentum.

The Recurring Lock

Turn a one-time "discovery" meeting into a permanent, shared roadmap review. One-off conversations are a start; they are not a partnership. Scheduling a recurring slot, such as a monthly roadmap sync or quarterly planning, makes the collaboration structural. The recurrence signals that you are committing, not just trying.

Public Attribution

Credit a specific win to an insight provided by a member of another team in front of executives."The documentation fix that reduced Support tickets came from what Roland's team told us in Q2." This behavior does two things: it closes the loop publicly, and it gives the other team visible credit. It builds trust with them and models cross-functional recognition for the organization.

The "Audit" Check

Explicitly ask, "Does this process feel like a partnership or an audit?" and listen to the answer. At Level 3, your intent may not match their perception. The audit check is a meta-conversation that surfaces the gap. If they say "audit," you have a chance to reframe, share your intent, and adjust. If you never ask, you may never know until they disengage.

How to Avoid Sliding Back

The risk here is that the friction of investigation causes the leader to seek the safety of the "Receptive" stage.

Language Risks

Unexplained Interrogation

Asking for data without providing the context or intent behind the request. When you ask "Can you send me your process?" without saying why, the other team fills in the blank with "audit" or "critique." Always preface with the problem you are solving and how their input will be used. Unexplained requests are a fast track back to suspicion.

Acronym Blindness

Using Home Team shorthand in mixed meetings without defining it. Your "MVP" or "SLA" may not mean the same thing to Marketing or Support. When you use an acronym in a mixed room, define it or ask if everyone is on the same page. Acronym blindness excludes people and reinforces the sense that you are still speaking "your" language, not "ours."

The "Yes, But" Reflex

Responding to a constraint with a justification instead of a question. When someone says "We can't do that because of X," the "Yes, but we need it" response shuts down the conversation. The Investigating response is "What would need to be true for X to change?" or "Help me understand X so we can find a path together." Justification defends; curiosity builds.

Othering Language

Referring to the partner group as "They" or "Them" in private meetings. Once you have a name and a relationship, use it."Roland's team" or "Sales" is more specific than "they." In private, "they" can slip back in, and that slip reinforces the mental wall between "us" and "them." Catch yourself and use the name.

Vague Commitments

Ending a hard talk with "We'll look into it" instead of a time-bound next step."We'll look into it" sounds like a brush-off. It does not close the loop or set an expectation. Replace it with "I'll come back to you by [date] with what we decided and how your input shaped it." The time-bound commitment helps keep the door open.

Behavioral Risks

The Extraction Pattern

Gathering data from another team but failing to provide an update within 14 days. If you learn something from them and act on it, they need to see it. Fourteen days is a reasonable window to close the loop by sending the "You Said, We Did" or the update that shows their input mattered. Beyond that, silence reads as extraction, and trust erodes.

Priority Cancellation

Dropping a cross-functional meeting because "internal fires" feel more urgent. At Level 3, the cross-functional meeting is not optional; it is the bridge you are building. When you cancel it for internal priorities, you signal that the partnership is still secondary. One cancellation may be forgiven; a pattern tells them where they stand. Protect the recurring lock.

The Surprise Drop

Making a decision that impacts another team without a pre-alert. When you change a timeline, a scope, or a deliverable that affects them, they should hear it from you before they hear it in a report or a hallway conversation. The surprise drop undermines the trust you have built and reinforces the sense that you are still operating in a silo. Pre-alert when your decisions touch their world.

Perfectionism Hiding

Withholding a draft because it "isn't polished," which stops early feedback. At Level 3, the goal is co-creation, not approval of a finished product. When you hold back the messy draft, you deny the other team the chance to shape it. Invite them into the mess; that is when their input is most valuable and when the partnership deepens.

Correction Over Curiosity

Using a joint meeting to "correct" others' views rather than to learn their reality. When they describe a process or a constraint differently than you understand it, the temptation is to set them straight. The Investigating stance is to assume their reality is valid and to ask questions until you understand it. Correction closes the door; curiosity keeps it open.

Level 4: Deciding (The Connected Leader)

Executive Summary

The "Deciding" leader eliminates the "Negotiation Tax." This hidden tax is the time and energy wasted bargaining over resources for every single project. By committing to a shared identity, they unlock "Compound Speed," where trust help teams execute without constant realignment.

Strategic Concepts

1. ***The Conscious Choice:*** *Collaboration is not a mood; it is a decision. Leaders must explicitly declare the end of the silo and the beginning of the shared unit.*
2. ***Crisis Reveals Reflexes:*** *When pressure hits, teams instinctively revert to old habits (blame and defense). The leader's primary job is to override this "muscle memory" during the first fire.*
3. ***The "Despite" Narrative:*** *In many companies, success happens despite the system. Deciding leaders reject this; they ensure success happens because of the shared system.*
4. ***Identity Fusion:*** *The goal is to stop being two functional teams (e.g. , "Sales" and "Ops") and become one value-stream team ("Revenue").*
5. ***Escalation creates Debt:*** *Going over a peer's head to solve a problem fixes the immediate issue but bankrupts the long-term relationship.*

Tactical Actions

1. ***The Zero-Sum Sacrifice**: Voluntarily cut a line item from your own budget to fund a critical need for a partner team.*
2. ***The United Front**: Agree on decisions privately so you never debate your counterpart in front of the both teams.*
3. ***The "We" Mandate**: In a crisis, forbid the use of the partner team's name. Use only "We" to describe the failure (e.g. , "We had a configuration drift").*
4. ***Open Kitchen**: Grant the partner team full view-access to your internal project boards and calendars. Secrets build walls.*
5. ***One Metric**: Establish a single "North Star" goal that requires both teams to succeed for anyone to claim victory.*

The Line in the Sand

Background

The day Vanessa Reyes declared that her team and the Infrastructure group were "one unit now," half of her engineers thought she had lost her mind.

She had gathered her entire Application Development team in the largest conference room at Coastal Dynamics. Joining them along the opposite wall were fourteen members of the Infrastructure team. The two groups had been at each other's throats for years.

"I want to be clear about something," Vanessa said."What has happened in the past is in the past. The finger-pointing, the blame games, the throw-it-over-the-wall mentality. That ends today. From this moment forward, we succeed together or we fail together. There is no 'your problem' or 'my problem. ' There is only 'our problem. '"

She had spent a month negotiating what this partnership would look like. Shared metrics. Joint planning sessions. A unified escalation path. But agreements on paper were one thing. Making them real was another.

"I know this feels strange. Some of you have been fighting with Infrastructure for so long that you have forgotten what it is like to work with them. But I am asking you to trust me. This is going to be hard. We are going to stumble. But I have made a decision that this is how we operate now. And I intend to hold that line."

The room was quiet.

Nobody clapped, but nobody argued either.

The Flashpoint

The test came two weeks later. The company's main customer portal went down at 2:47 PM on a Friday.

Both teams mobilized. By 4:00 PM, the problem had been isolated. A database connection pool was exhausting itself due to a recent code change. It was, technically, an Application Development issue.

When Vanessa joined the incident call, she could already feel the old dynamics trying to reassert themselves.

"This is exactly what we warned about," said one of the Infrastructure leads."The code was not properly load-tested before deployment."

"The test procedures were not realistic," shot back one of Vanessa's developers."We test what we can with what we have."

Vanessa felt a familiar weight in her chest. This was the exact moment where partnerships died. She could feel both teams reaching for the comfort of "us versus them."

She unmuted her microphone.

"Stop."The channel went quiet.

"I hear what is happening right now. When things go wrong, the instinct is to protect ourselves. To point at someone else and say 'that is on them. ' But that instinct is exactly what got us into this mess in the first place. Years of blame-shifting. Years of walls. And what did it get us? A system so fragile that one bad query pattern can take down our entire portal."

She let that sink in.

"We are going to fix this outage together. Not App Dev fixing 'our' bug while Infrastructure watches. We are going to solve this as one team. And when it is over, we are going to do a blameless post-mortem."

The outage was resolved by 8:00 PM. In the post-mortem that followed, instead of pointing fingers, both teams pointed at systems. They identified gaps in testing infrastructure, the communication breakdowns in deployment, and monitoring blind spots.

It was not perfect. But for the first time, the teams worked through the friction instead of retreating from it.

The Daily Discipline

What surprised Vanessa most was not the big moments. Everyone knew they were being watched when there was a production outage.

The real challenge was the small stuff.

Three weeks later, Vanessa was walking past the break room when she overheard two developers talking.

"And then Infrastructure changed the firewall rules without telling anyone. Classic Infrastructure move."

Vanessa paused. Her first instinct was to keep walking. It was just venting. But she caught herself. This was exactly the kind of thing that eroded partnerships. The small complaints. The casual blame. The "us vs. them" language that seemed harmless until it hardened into something toxic.

She stepped into the break room.

"Hey. What happened with the firewall rules?"

The developers looked startled."Oh, it was nothing major. Just a miscommunication. Already fixed."

"But I noticed you said 'classic Infrastructure move." Did you reach out to figure out a better process for next time?"

"Well, no."

"So the problem was solved, but the relationship was not. The frustration is still there. And now it is coming out as 'classic Infrastructure move' instead of 'here is a communication gap we need to address. '"

She sat down with them.

"The language we use matters, even when we think no one is listening. When we say 'classic Infrastructure move,' we are reinforcing the idea that they are fundamentally different from us. Start with curiosity instead of blame. Reach out and ask what happened. Either way, you are building a connection instead of tearing one down."

The Decision

Six months in, Vanessa noticed something troubling. The partnership was holding. But it was also exhausting her.

Every day felt like a battle against gravity. Left to their own devices, both teams drifted back toward isolation. Old habits resurfaced in small ways. Every time, Vanessa had to intervene.

It was like the organization had muscle memory for fighting. She could tell people they were one team, but their reflexes were still wired for conflict.

But she had made a decision. And she intended to keep making it. Tomorrow. And the day after. And every day for as long as she wanted this to work.

The choice was not behind her. It was ahead of her.

She would keep making it.

Breaking It Down

Leaders at the Deciding level act as the "Connected" archetype. This stage is a major tipping point: the leader has moved past just looking around and is now choosing to adopt a shared identity with other groups. They are better at sharing visions that work for everyone, and they show a real commitment to staying connected. While collaboration is clearly growing, silos still pop up now and then. This means the leader must keep choosing to connect until it becomes a habit.

The Home Team's Language

At this stage, the leader is good at using "constructive" language to set goals that make sense to many groups. They have mostly stopped using the "us vs. them" talk of the past. However, because this is a transition phase, the new way of speaking isn't second nature yet. The leader might still have moments where they lack clarity and have to stop and correct themselves to keep building bridges instead of walls.

Bridge-Building Behaviors

Leader behaviors at this level are firmly toward COLLABORATING. The leader has moved from ISOLATING toward COLLABORATING and is actively reinforcing shared outcomes. They prioritize working together through joint planning and shared projects. Even though they are making progress, some obstacles still appear. The leader must find and fix these new barriers to prove their commitment is real.

The Language Building Zone

Level 4 is the pivotal moment in the Language Building Zone. The leader has "decided" to work together, but the company's old habit of staying isolated is still strong. Here, the leader's words prove that their decision is solid. When things get tough, The Home Team looks at the leader's language to see if they are actually staying the course or just going through a phase. The leader must use their words to override the old instinct to hide in a silo during stress.

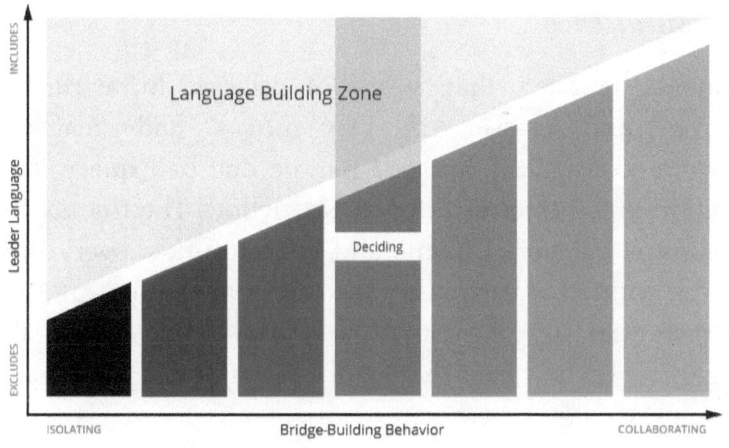

Level 4: Deciding (The Connected Leader)

The Lesson: Holding the Line

Vanessa's story shows that a partnership only becomes real when it survives a crisis.

The Home Team Trap

When the portal went down, both teams reached for the "us vs. them" script. Vanessa's own developers tried to blame another team (Infrastructure) to protect themselves. The trap is assuming that under pressure people will remember the new identity; they won't unless the leader names the reflex and redirects it in real time.

The Silent Thief

Vanessa realized that years of "classic Infrastructure moves" and "classic App Dev moves" had created a system so fragile it couldn't handle one bad query. This friction is the thief of Friction Reduction. The thief is the accumulated cost of blame and workarounds: every time teams pointed at each other instead of at the system, they added debt. By the time the portal went down, the organization had paid that tax for years in rework, delays, and lost trust.

The Echo Chamber

Even in the break room, Vanessa had to stop her team from "venting." She knew that casual blame is a weed that eventually chokes the whole garden. What feels like harmless relief in the moment, such as the thought "classic Infrastructure move," reinforces the very walls the leader is trying to tear down. The echo chamber is the private space where the old identity gets rehearsed; if the leader doesn't interrupt it, the public commitment will erode from the inside.

The Pivot: Changing the Script

The pivot here shows how Vanessa used Bridge-Building language to stop the blame game and focus on the Collective Intelligence of the whole unit.

The Script Shift

Vanessa refused to let her team retreat to their "corners". She used the Story of Us to force a shared victory:

"Stop. I hear the instinct to point fingers, but that is what got us here. We are not App Dev fixing 'our' bug while Infrastructure watches. We are solving this as one team, and we will do a blameless review together when it's over. We succeed or fail as one unit now."

Reviewing the Deciding Level

A leader at the Deciding level has made a choice but must still guard against old reflexes. Look for these performance "leaks":

The "Contractual" Phrase

Using words that imply you are helping another team because you "promised" rather than because it is a shared goal. When you frame support as a favor or a trade, you reinforce the idea that you are two teams with a deal, not one unit with a shared outcome. The contractual phrase keeps the relationship transactional; the Deciding leader speaks in terms of "we" and "our goal" so the commitment reads as identity, not obligation.

Possessive Regression

Slipping back into saying "My budget" or "My roadmap" instead of "Our capacity." At Level 4, resources are shared in spirit even if they are still allocated by function. When you say "my" in front of your team or your counterpart, you signal that the silo is still the default. Catch yourself and reframe: "our capacity," "our roadmap," "our timeline." The words shape how both sides see the partnership.

The "Despite" Narrative

Allowing your team to claim a win happened "despite" the red tape of another group. That narrative credits your team and discredits the other. It preserves the idea that success happens in spite of the system rather than because of it. The Deciding leader corrects the record: "We hit the goal because we aligned with Ops on the timeline" reframes the other team as necessary support, not obstacle.

Shadow Workarounds

Letting the Home Team build secret processes to avoid following shared rules. When the going gets hard, the reflex is to route around the other team. This could be a separate spreadsheet, a back-channel approval, or a "just this once" exception. Each workaround undermines the shared system and teaches both sides that the formal partnership is optional. The Deciding leader surfaces and dismantles workarounds so the one-unit identity is reflected in how work actually runs.

The Escalation Bypass

Going over a peer's head to their boss to win an argument rather than solving it with them. Escalation fixes the immediate issue but creates debt: the peer feels undermined, and the next time they will be less likely to collaborate. The Deciding leader keeps conflict within the partnership and uses the united front to resolve it, even when it would be faster to escalate.

How Vanessa Levels Up

To move to the Grounded level, Vanessa must move from "making the choice" to "living the reality". She must synchronize both groups until they move in lockstep.

Listen for this Language

The Narrative Correction

When a team member says a win happened "despite" another group, explicitly correct the record to frame them as necessary support. One sentence can reset the narrative: "We couldn't have hit that deadline without Ops clearing the change window." The correction is not scolding; it is teaching the group how to speak about the partnership so the identity sticks.

The "One Voice" Mandate

Co-author all major updates with your counterpart so the message comes from the "Combined Leadership Team." When both leaders sign the same message, the organization sees one unit. When they send separate memos, they see two teams that happen to coordinate. The one voice mandate makes the shared identity visible in every communication.

The "We" Absolute

In a crisis, strictly forbid using another team's name; use only "We" to describe the collective group."We had a configuration drift" is different from "App Dev had a configuration drift." The "we" forces accountability and identity into the same sentence. It's the linguistic equivalent of holding the line.

Value-Based Defense

When the other group makes a mistake, describe it as a "system failure" rather than "incompetence." Blame attaches to people; system failure attaches to process, tools, or communication. The Deciding leader redirects the conversation so the post-mortem helps to improve the system instead of scarring the relationship."Our deployment checks didn't catch this" keeps the unit intact.

The Shared Destiny

Articulate one "North Star" metric that requires both teams to succeed to hit their year. When the goal is shared, success and failure are shared. The shared destiny makes it impossible to claim a win that leaves the other team behind. It gives both sides a single sentence to repeat when the old reflexes kick in.

Behaviors to Observe

The Zero-Sum Sacrifice

Voluntarily cut an item from your own budget to fund a critical need for another team that helps the shared goal. The sacrifice is visible proof that you are not optimizing for your silo. It signals that the North Star matters more than your team's slice of the pie. One sacrifice can do more for trust than a dozen speeches.

The "Open Kitchen" Policy

Grant the other team full view-access to your internal project boards and calendars. Secrets build walls; transparency builds shared context. When the other team can see your priorities and your capacity without asking, they can align without negotiating. The open kitchen turns the partnership from a handshake into a shared operating system.

The United Front

Agree on a decision privately with your counterpart so you never disagree in front of the combined teams. Public disagreement (even on small things) gives both teams permission to pick sides again. The united front means the two leaders have already merged; the teams see one decision, one message, one unit.

The Talent Swap

Temporarily embed a member of the Home Team into another team for a full project. The swap builds empathy, transfers knowledge, and makes the "one unit" idea tangible. When people work inside the other team's context, they stop seeing them as "them" and start seeing the shared constraints. It is a high-commitment behavior that accelerates the shift to Grounded.

The Blameless Joint Review

Host a retrospective where individual teams cannot be named as the "cause" of a failure, only shared systems. When the review names systems (deployment checks, communication protocols, escalation paths) instead of people or teams, the outcome is learning, not blame, and the partnership stays intact.

How to Avoid Sliding Back

The risk here is that the "muscle memory" for conflict pulls the leader back into a state of just "Investigating" or "Receptive".

Language Risks

Transactional Framing

Framing a request as a trade ("I'll do X if you do Y") instead of a shared mission. Trades keep the relationship bilateral and conditional. The Deciding leader frames requests in terms of the shared goal: "We need X to hit our North Star" invites the other team into the same mission. If you slip into "if you do this, we'll do that," you have stepped back from identity into negotiation.

Passive-Aggressive Compliance

Using language like "We are doing exactly what they asked for" to distance yourself from a potential failure. The phrase signals that you are executing their plan, not owning the outcome. When the project fails, "they asked for it" is ready as an exit. The Deciding leader says "we committed to this" so that success and failure are shared.

The "Yes, But" Habit

Responding to a partner's problem with an immediate justification rather than an inquiry."Yes, but we had constraints" closes the door."Help me understand what you needed, what would have made it work?" keeps it open. Justification defends your team; inquiry builds the partnership. At Level 4, the default response to a complaint is curiosity, not defense.

Possessive Drift

Letting the words "My guys" or "My staff" creep back into resource talks."My" reasserts ownership and boundaries. In the Deciding stage, the goal is "our capacity," "our people," "our timeline," language that reflects the shared identity. Catch possessive drift early; it is often the first sign that the old reflexes are resurfacing.

Unexplained Interrogation

Asking "Why are you doing that?" without giving the context of why the answer matters for the shared goal. Without context, the question sounds like a challenge or an audit. When you need to understand the other team's choices, preface with the shared goal: "To align our timelines, I need to understand why that step is there." Context turns the question into collaboration.

Behavioral Risks

The "Real Meeting" After-Party

Holding a separate meeting with just your team after a joint session to vent or complain. The after-party is where the old identity gets rehearsed. What wasn't said in the room gets said in the hallway, and that conversation often undermines the united front. The Deciding leader either addresses concerns in the room or commits to not rehearsing them in private. If you need to debrief, frame it as "how we support the shared outcome," not "what they did wrong."

The "Wobble" Ignore

Noticing a small process failure and choosing to ignore it, allowing a bad habit to start. One missed handoff, one exception to the shared rule, one "just this once" can become the new normal. The Deciding leader treats small wobbles as early warnings. Naming and fixing them before they spread is how the partnership stays real when the spotlight is off.

Resource Hoarding

Hiding budget or time surplus to ensure the Home Team has a "buffer" the other group doesn't know about. Hoarding is the behavioral version of possessive language: it keeps "our" resources separate from "theirs." The Deciding leader makes capacity visible so both teams can plan against the same reality. A hidden buffer is a wall in disguise.

Curated Transparency

Sharing a "cleaned up" PDF report rather than a link to the live, messy data. The PDF is a snapshot that invites questions; the live link is an invitation to see the same reality. Curated transparency says "we'll show you what we want you to see." Full transparency says "we work in the same kitchen." The Deciding leader shares the messy source so the other team can trust what they see.

Priority Cancellation

At Level 4, the joint meeting is not optional; it is the structure that holds the partnership. When you cancel it for internal priorities, you signal that the shared rhythm is still secondary. One cancellation may be forgiven; a pattern tells the other team where they stand. Protect the recurring lock.

Level 5: Grounded (The Aligned Leader)

Executive Summary

The "Grounded" leader eliminates the "Alignment Tax." This hidden tax is the constant need to re-litigate decisions between departments. By stabilizing the partnership, they turn cross-functional friction into "Resilience."

Strategic Concepts

1. ***Orchestration vs. Coordination****: The goal shifts from "checking in" with partners to moving in lockstep. The partnership is no longer a series of meetings; instead it is a shared rhythm.*
2. ***The Stabilizing Force****: Language is no longer just a tool for change; it is a tool for maintenance. The leader uses consistent vocabulary to keep the "Us vs. Them" weeds from growing back.*
3. ***Crisis Resilience****: The true test of this level is not success; it is failure. When bad news hits, Grounded teams solve the problem together instead of retreating to their corners to assign blame.*
4. ***No Daylight****: Leaders may debate fiercely in private, but they present a 100% unified front in public. To the team, there is no "R&D View" vs. "Ops View." There is only the "Leadership View."*
5. ***Maintenance****: The work is no longer about construction; it is about stewardship. The leader must vigilantly tend the relationship to prevent complacency.*

Tactical Actions

1. ***The Single Roadmap***: *Abolish separate functional roadmaps. Create one master document grouped by business outcome, not by department.*
2. ***Talent Swaps***: *Embed a high-potential lead in the partner team for a 90-day rotation to build empathy and system knowledge.*
3. ***Governance Merger***: *Combine separate weekly review boards into a single decision-making body.*
4. ***The "No-Handoff" Rule***: *Ban words like "handoff" or "transfer." Describe the work as a continuous loop owned by the collective group.*
5. ***The Uncomfortable Question***: *Publicly ask your partner: "What is my team doing that makes your job hard?" and listen without defending.*

The Shared Ground

Background

When people asked Evelyn Matsuda how long the partnership between Clinical Operations and Research & Development had been working, she had to stop and think about it. Two years? Two and a half? The exact date had blurred because at some point, the collaboration had simply become the way things were done at Castellex Therapeutics.

Evelyn led Clinical Operations, the team responsible for running the human trials that turned promising compounds into approved medicines. For most of the company's history, her group and R&D had existed in cautious distance. R&D created the science and Clinical Ops tested it on people. The handoff between them was formal, documented, and marked by many small frictions.

That changed over the past two years. The transformation had not been dramatic. It had been a slow buildup of shared work, shared language, and shared accountability. Until one day Evelyn realized she could not remember the last time she had thought of R&D as "the other side." They were just the team. Different functions, same mission.

The Monday Rhythm

Every Monday morning at 8:30, Evelyn joined the combined leadership meeting that had become the heartbeat of both organizations. Twelve people sat mixed together, not in opposing rows. A seating arrangement that had evolved naturally over time.

Omar, the SVP of R&D, sat at the head of the table with Evelyn. They had developed a habit of co-facilitating these sessions, passing the conversational baton back and forth without explicit coordination.

Evelyn noticed how naturally her directors included R&D colleagues in their updates. Not as a courtesy, but as a given. Years ago, a conversation like this would have required a formal meeting request, a negotiation about agenda items, and probably some posturing about whose timeline took priority.

Now it was just Monday.

The Language of "We"

Later that morning, Evelyn met with her direct reports.

"I want to talk about something I noticed in the Monday meeting," she said."When you mentioned the enrollment lag, you said 'our site management team' and then referenced R&D's group. Two years ago, you would have said 'my team is handling the sites, and I have reached out to R&D for input. ' The framing would have been us-and-them. Today, you talked about both groups as if they were part of the same operation."

"I didn't notice I was doing that," one of her directors admitted.

"That is exactly my point. It has become natural. But I want us to be conscious of it. The way we talk shapes the way we think. If we keep using language that treats R&D as part of our shared effort, we reinforce that reality. If we slip back into 'us and them,' even casually, we start to erode it."

The Test

Three weeks later, the Phase 2 readout arrived. It was not what anyone had hoped for.

The trial had shown clear efficacy, but the safety profile was more complex than expected. Three patients had experienced a rare cardiac event. While none were life-threatening, the pattern was enough to raise a regulatory flag. The FDA would want answers before any Phase 3 could proceed.

By 7:15 AM, Evelyn was on the phone with Omar."We need to get the team together. Not just leadership. I want the clinical leads and the research scientists in the same room, looking at the same data."

The meeting that followed was tense but focused. Evelyn and Omar sat side by side, facilitating a discussion that ranged across pharmacology, patient selection, and cardiac physiology. At one point, the conversation grew heated. A scientist from R&D challenged the methodology of the safety assessment. One of Evelyn's medical directors pushed back sharply.

Evelyn intervened."Hold on. Let us remember why we are here. We have unexpected data that we need to understand. That is not a failure. It is science. The question is not who did something wrong. It's "What are we seeing and what do we do about it?"

She looked at both of them."I need us to be curious instead of defensive. Assume good faith. Assume we are all trying to solve the same problem. Because we are."

The room settled. By the end of the meeting, they had a plan. A deep-dive analysis, a protocol amendment, and a joint communication to the FDA. Every action item was assigned to a cross-functional pair to ensure the response was unified.

"When we talk about this externally," Omar said, "we speak with one voice. There is no 'R&D's position' and 'Clinical's position. ' There is Castellex's position."

The Steady Foundation

One afternoon, after the crisis had passed, one of her newer directors stopped by Evelyn's office.

"During the crisis, I kept waiting for the partnership to break down. Every other company I have worked at, a setback like that would have triggered a blame war. But it did not happen here. Why?"

Evelyn considered the question."Because we have been building something for two years that is bigger than any single project. The partnership is not based on one trial succeeding. It is based on a shared understanding of how we work together. When the setback hit, people defaulted to that understanding instead of retreating to their corners."

"Does that take constant effort?"

"Yes and no. Two years ago, every conversation felt like effort. I had to consciously choose every word. Now it is more like maintenance than construction. The foundation is solid. I still have to tend to it. But I am not building from scratch anymore. I am protecting something that already exists."

Breaking It Down

Leaders at the Grounded level act as the "Aligned" archetype. At this stage, the awkwardness of earlier levels disappears, and the partnership is built on a shared reality. These leaders use a unified approach to communication, ensuring their message sounds the same to every group. They have aligned their vision and values with another team, creating a shared sense of purpose. The relationship is no longer just about stopping fights; it is about moving in total sync toward mutual goals.

The Home Team's Language

At this level, the leader has polished their language so it resonates with everyone. Using "constructive" language is now the standard way of doing business, not a difficult choice. The leader's words act as a stabilizing force that keeps "us vs. them" stories from coming back. Their communication is reliable and unified, which makes everyone feel safe.

Bridge-Building Behaviors

Behaviors at this level are arriving at or firmly at COLLABORATING. The leader has moved from ISOLATING toward COLLABORATING and now ensures different groups move in lockstep toward shared goals. The old shadows of silos begin to fade as collaborative habits, like joint roadmapping, become part of the daily routine. While the work is not yet "seamless," there is a strong sense of shared responsibility across old boundaries.

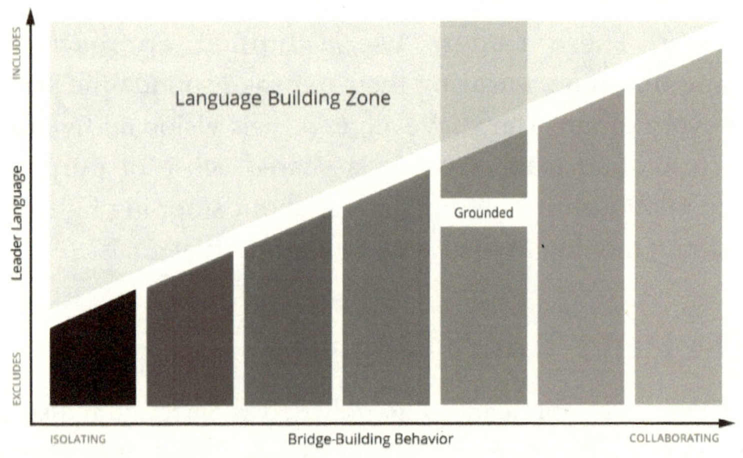

Level 5: Grounded (The Aligned Leader)

The Language Building Zone

Level 5 is a stabilizing moment in the Language Building Zone. The massive gap between words and actions begins to level out. Because bridge-building is now consistent, the relationship is "grounded" in trust. Actions now speak as loudly as words, so the leader's language doesn't have to do all the heavy lifting anymore. The goal shifts from creating trust to maintaining alignment through consistency.

The Lesson: The Shared Ground

Evelyn's story shows that a "Grounded" partnership survives even when the data is bad.

The Home Team Trap

In the past, a safety failure like the one in CTX-401 would have triggered a "blame war" between Clinical and R&D. When the Phase 2 readout showed unexpected cardiac events, the old reflex would have been to point at the other function: R&D at Clinical's trial design, Clinical at R&D's compound profile. The trap is assuming that under pressure the partnership will hold without the leader explicitly redirecting the conversation. At Grounded, the leader names the reflex and keeps the focus on the problem, not the blame.

The Silent Thief

Evelyn realized that assigning blame is a thief of Collective Intelligence. By framing the failure as "Our hypothesis didn't pan out," she protected the organization's energy. The thief is the energy spent on defensiveness and finger-pointing instead of on learning. When the leader reframes a setback as a shared hypothesis that did not pan out, the team can channel that energy into analysis and next steps rather than into protecting turf.

The Echo Chamber

Even when a new executive arrived with old "us vs. them" habits, the existing culture was strong enough to redirect her. The "ground" was already set. At Level 5, the partnership has been reinforced for long enough that the culture itself acts as a corrective. New members may slip into old language, but the norms and the leader's consistency pull them back. The echo chamber is less likely to form because the default is already "we."

The Pivot: Changing the Script

The pivot here shows how Evelyn used Bridge-Building language to keep the team focused on science instead of defense. When the meeting grew heated, she stopped the friction immediately.

The Script Shift

Evelyn used the Story of Us to turn a technical crisis into a shared learning moment:

"Hold on. We have unexpected data, and we need to understand it. That is not a failure; it is science. The question isn't who did something wrong. It's "What are we seeing, and what do we do about it together?" I need us to be curious instead of defensive. Assume we're all solving the same problem, because we are."

Reviewing the Grounded Level

A leader at the Grounded level has built a foundation but must still maintain it. Look for these performance "leaks":

Laned Success

Describing a win as "our team did their part and another team did theirs," which reinforces separate lanes instead of a shared victory. When you credit the outcome to two separate contributions, you preserve the mental model of two teams. The Grounded leader describes the win as "we hit the goal" or "our joint effort delivered," so the victory is owned collectively. Laned success language keeps the identity split when it should be fused.

The Polite Deferral

Saying "I can't speak to that" rather than attempting to answer based on the shared context you've built. At Level 5, you have enough shared context to speak for the partnership on many topics. When you defer every question about the other team's domain, you signal that the walls are still there. The polite deferral is a small leak that says "that's their territory, not ours." Try to answer from shared knowledge, or say "Let me confirm with [counterpart] and we'll get back as one."

The "Guest" Dynamic

Using words that imply another team is just "visiting" your space rather than co-owning the work. Language like "they're joining our meeting" or "we're hosting them" keeps the other team in a guest role. The Grounded leader says "our meeting" and "our space" so that both teams are owners. The guest dynamic is a subtle regression that reintroduces host and visitor, and with it, the expectation that one side has more claim than the other.

Possessive Drift

Slipping back into "My guys" or "My staff" when talking about resources. At Level 5, the goal is "our capacity," "our people," "our timeline." When you say "my" in front of your team in a joint context, you reassert boundaries that the partnership has been working to soften. Catch possessive drift early; it is often the first sign that stress is pulling the leader back toward silo language.

The Client/Vendor Frame

Treating the output of a partner as a "delivery" you are "accepting" rather than a shared creation. When you talk about "receiving" their work or "signing off" on it, you cast them as suppliers and yourself as a client. The Grounded leader describes the work as co-created: "we delivered," "we built," "we shipped." The client/vendor frame reintroduces a power dynamic that undermines the shared identity.

How Evelyn Levels Up

To move to the Embedded level, Evelyn must move beyond synchronization toward deep integration. Collaboration must become the default state of existence.

Listen for this Language

The "No-Handoff" Narrative

Stop using words like "transfer" or "toss." Describe the work as a continuous loop owned by the group. When you eliminate handoff language, you eliminate the mental model of discrete batches of work moving between teams. The "no-handoff" narrative reframes the work as one flow, one ownership. It is a linguistic shift that supports the behavioral shift to Embedded.

Cross-Domain Advocacy

In budget meetings, advocate for another team's needs using their own technical arguments. When you speak for their priorities in their terms, you signal that you have internalized their reality. You are not just supporting them; you are representing them. Cross-domain advocacy is a high-trust behavior that shows the partnership has moved from coordination to true integration.

The "We" Stress Test

During a failure, refuse to blame a specific department. Insist that "Our joint architecture is what allowed a failure mode." The stress test is whether you can hold the "we" when the stakes are high. When something goes wrong, the old reflex is to identify whose fault it was. The Grounded leader keeps the frame on the system: our process, our architecture, our joint design. That reframe protects the partnership when it is most at risk.

Identity Blending

Create a single project name for the combined effort and stop using functional team names. When the initiative has one name, such as "Project Meridian," instead of "R&D's trial" and "Clinical's execution," the identity blends. People start to say "we're on Meridian" instead of "we're from Clinical" or "we're from R&D." Identity blending is a small change with that has a large effect on how the team sees itself.

The "Uncomfortable" Question

Publicly ask the partner team, "What is my team doing that makes your job harder?" and listen without defending. The question is uncomfortable because it invites criticism in front of others. But it also signals that you want to improve the partnership, not protect your turf. When you ask it and then act on the answer, you close the loop and deepen trust.

Behaviors to Observe

The "Single Source" Roadmap

Abolish separate team roadmaps. Use one document grouped by business outcomes. When there is one roadmap, there is one plan. When there are two, there are two teams. The single source forces alignment and makes it visible. It is a structural commitment that the work is shared between teams.

Talent Exchange

Send a high-potential member of the Home Team to work inside another team for 90 days. The rotation builds empathy, transfers knowledge, and makes the "one unit" idea tangible. When people work inside the other team's context, they stop seeing them as "them" and start seeing the shared constraints. Talent commingling accelerates the shift from Grounded to Embedded.

Shared Reward Structures

Propose that leadership bonuses be tied to the exact same shared metric. When success is measured the same way for both leaders, the incentive to optimize for one's own silo drops. Shared reward structures align behavior with the shared identity. It is a high-commitment signal that the partnership is not optional.

The "Open Door" Strategy

Give the partner team full edit access to your team's strategic planning documents. When they can edit, not just view, the boundary between "our plan" and "their plan" disappears. The open door strategy turns transparency into co-ownership. It is a trust accelerator that only works when the foundation is already Grounded.

Governance Merger

Combine separate review boards into a single decision-making body. When one board reviews both teams' work, the decisions are made in a shared context. Governance merger eliminates the "we present to them" dynamic and replaces it with "we present to us." It is a structural behavior that reinforces the one-unit identity.

How to Avoid Sliding Back

The risk here is assuming the alignment is permanent and stopping the daily work of "tending the garden".

Language Risks

The "Contractual" Phrasing

Saying "I promised I'd help" (doing it for them) instead of "We need to solve this" (doing it for us). When you frame support as a promise or a favor, you keep the relationship bilateral. The Grounded leader frames it as a shared need: "we need to solve this" keeps the identity intact. Contractual phrasing is a small slip that reintroduces the notion of "you" and "me" where "we" should be.

Possessive Regression

Reverting to "My budget" or "My headcount" during stressful resource talks. Under pressure, the old language returns."My" reasserts ownership and boundaries. The Grounded leader catches the slip and reframes: "our capacity," "our headcount," "our budget." Possessive regression is an early warning that the leader is under stress and may be retreating toward silo thinking.

The "Despite" Narrative

Allowing a team member to joke about a partner's "slowness" without challenging the comment. When someone says "we got it done despite Ops" or laughs at a partner's process, the leader must correct the record. Letting it slide reinforces the idea that the other team is an obstacle. The Grounded leader names it: "We got it done with Ops. Let's keep the narrative aligned."

Transactional Framing

Framing a request as a trade rather than a requirement for the shared mission."If you do X, we'll do Y" keeps the relationship conditional. The Grounded leader frames requests in terms of the shared goal: "We need X to hit our North Star" invites the other team into the same mission. Transactional framing is a step back from identity into negotiation.

Passive-Aggressive Compliance

Saying "We are doing exactly what they asked" to distance your team from a possible failure. The phrase signals that you are executing their plan, not owning the outcome. When the project fails, "they asked for it" is ready as an exit. The Grounded leader says "we committed to this" so that success and failure are shared. Passive-aggressive compliance reintroduces the us-them boundary at the moment it matters most.

Behavioral Risks

The "Pre-Meeting" Meeting

Holding a strategy session with only your team to align on a story before meeting the partner. The pre-meeting creates a unified "us" that then faces "them" in the joint session. It is the behavioral equivalent of possessive language: we have our position, they have theirs. The Grounded leader either co-creates the position with the counterpart in advance or enters the joint meeting without a pre-aligned "story" so the conversation is truly shared.

Curated Transparency

Sharing a "cleaned up" version of a report rather than giving a link to the live, messy data. The cleaned version says "we'll show you what we want you to see." The live link says "we work in the same kitchen." At Level 5, the default should be full transparency. Curated transparency is a regression that rebuilds a wall both teams had worked to take down.

Siloed Onboarding

Training a new hire without a module dedicated to the partner team's function. When new people join your team and learn only your side of the partnership, they inherit the old mental model. Siloed onboarding reproduces the silo in the next generation. The Grounded leader ensures that onboarding includes the partner team's context, goals, and how the two groups work together.

Unilateral Optimization

Changing a tool within your team to "move faster" without seeing how it breaks the shared workflow. When you optimize your piece without considering the joint process, you may speed up your team while slowing down the whole. Unilateral optimization is a leak that says "our efficiency matters more than our alignment." The Grounded leader checks with their partner before changing tools or processes that touch or impact the shared workflow.

The "Escalation" Reversion

Going to your boss to "break a tie" rather than staying in the room until you reach a consensus with your peer. Escalation fixes the immediate decision but creates debt: the peer feels bypassed, and the next time they will be less likely to invest in the partnership. The Grounded leader stays in the room and works through the disagreement with the counterpart. Consensus may take longer, but it preserves the one-unit identity.

Level 6: Embedded (The Collaborative Leader)

Executive Summary

The "Embedded" leader eliminates the "Integration Tax." This hidden tax is the massive loss of momentum that occurs when new teams, acquisitions, or departments try to merge. By making collaboration the default state, they unlock "Adaptive Speed," allowing the organization to absorb new capabilities without breaking its stride.

Strategic Concepts

1. ***Default vs. Special**: At this level, collaboration ceases to be a "special initiative" or a "task force." It becomes the baseline for how normal work gets done.*
2. ***Integration ≠ Assimilation**: When a new group enters (like an acquisition), the goal is not to force them into the old mold ("This is how we do it"), but to co-author a new chapter ("How does this change us?").*
3. ***Narrative Stewardship**: Culture is not shaped by policies; it is shaped by the stories leaders tell. If you celebrate individual heroes, you get silos. If you celebrate collective wins, you get an ecosystem.*
4. ***The "Guest" Error**: Treating a partner team as "visitors" (even politely) reinforces the boundary. In an embedded system, there are no guests, only co-owners.*
5. ***Permeable Borders**: Talent, data, and budget must flow across functional lines. If resources are trapped in a department, the ecosystem starves.*

Tactical Actions

1. ***The Story Circle:*** *Establish a regular ritual dedicated solely to sharing stories of how teams collaborated, not just what they delivered.*
2. ***The Shadow Mandate:*** *Require every leader to complete a one-week rotation inside a partner department before they are eligible for promotion.*
3. ***Mixed Interviews:*** *Give a peer from a partner function the power to veto your new hires. If the new hires don't fit the ecosystem, they don't get the job.*
4. ***The Shared Wallet:*** *Create at least one budget line (e.g., "Innovation Fund") that requires a joint signature from two different functional leads to unlock.*
5. ***Kick it Back:*** *When a conflict arises, refuse to "break the tie." Send the teams back to the room and tell them to return only when they have a shared proposal.*

The Story We Tell

Background

There was a moment, about three years into the transformation, when Iris Delgado realized she had stopped thinking about it.

She was standing in the lobby of Barkdale Media Group's headquarters, watching a scene that would have been unthinkable five years earlier.

A production team from Documentary was clustered around a whiteboard with engineers from Streaming and marketers from Brand Partnerships.

They were sketching out a distribution strategy. Voices overlapping. Ideas building on ideas. There was no one waiting for permission or worrying about whose budget would cover what.

It was a Tuesday. It was ordinary. That, Iris understood, was the whole point.

As Chief Content Officer, Iris oversaw three divisions that had once operated as separate kingdoms. For years, they had competed for resources, blamed each other for failures, and celebrated wins in isolation.

Now she could not remember the last time someone had asked which division "owned" a project. The question had simply stopped being relevant.

The Story Circle

Every month, Iris hosted what had become known as the "Story Circle." A gathering of leaders from across her divisions. The format was simple. People shared stories. Not metrics, not status updates. Stories. The only rule was that every story had to be told as a collective narrative. Not "my team did this" but "here is what our teams discovered together."

This was what embedded collaboration looked like. Not a special initiative, but an organic integration that made the boundaries between groups feel almost arbitrary.

The Language of the Collective

Later that afternoon, Iris met with her executive team.

"I want to talk about something I have been noticing," she said, pulling up a slide showing recent internal communications.

"Our next step is to figure out how the streaming experience can amplify the live audience's engagement..."

"The creative vision we are developing together will require some new technical capabilities..."

"Do you notice what is missing? There is no 'my team' or 'your team. ' It is all 'we' and 'our. ' The language is not just reflecting reality. It is reinforcing it."

She leaned back."But here is what I am wondering. Are we maintaining the energy of this collective identity, or are we coasting on momentum? I have seen organizations reach this point and then slowly drift apart. People get comfortable, stop actively nurturing the connections, and one day they wake up in silos again."

The Flashpoint

The test came three months later, when Barkdale acquired a smaller production company called Firelight Studios.

Firelight had a sterling reputation for innovative content. The acquisition made strategic sense, but it presented a cultural challenge. Firelight had its own way of working, its own identity.

In the early discussions, Iris noticed something troubling. Her leaders were talking about Firelight as "them."

"We need to figure out how to use Firelight's talent on our projects," someone said.

"Once they understand how we work, they will be a great addition to our pipeline," another added.

The language was subtle, but Iris caught it. After years of building a culture where "we" meant everyone, her team was unconsciously drawing a line. Firelight was being positioned as outsiders who needed to be taught the Barkdale way.

She raised her hand.

"I am hearing a lot about what Firelight can do for us and how we will bring them into our processes. But I am not hearing about what we might learn from them. Or how our culture might evolve through integration."

The room shifted uncomfortably.

"We have spent years building something special here. But that culture is not static. It has to keep growing. If we treat Firelight as a team to be absorbed rather than partners to be embraced, we are not living up to what we have built. We are protecting it instead of extending it."

She looked around the table."Instead of asking 'how do we integrate Firelight into our way of working,' I want us to ask 'how will we work once Firelight is part of us?'"

The Integration

Iris approached the integration with deliberate intention. She started by spending time with the Firelight team. Not to explain Barkdale's culture, but to listen to theirs. She learned they called their brainstorming sessions "spark labs" and had a tradition of celebrating failures as collaborative learning moments.

Rather than imposing Barkdale's processes, Iris looked for ways to blend the best of both.

"What if we experimented with spark labs across all our divisions?" she suggested in a Story Circle that included both existing Barkdale employees and Firelight newcomers."Firelight has already figured out a format that works. Why not learn from them?"

She watched the Firelight team sit up straighter. Surprised to be positioned as teachers rather than students.

Within six months, the language had shifted. Firelight members had stopped referring to "the Barkdale way" and started saying "the way we work." When someone new joined, they encountered a culture that felt unified, not simply merged.

There was no sense of "old Barkdale" versus "new Firelight." There was just us.

The Story We Tell Ourselves

That evening, Iris reflected on what had happened. The culture she had built was not a fortress to be defended. It was a living thing that had to keep growing.

Keep telling the story. Keep using "we" instead of "they." Keep welcoming new people as co-authors who bring their own chapters.

The story only continues if we keep choosing to tell it.

Together.

Breaking It Down

The Home Team's Language

At this stage, the leader has mastered the art of resonant language. They move beyond just matching goals to sharing a vision that inspires action across different groups. The leader's messages work because they reflect the shared reality of the teams. Their language emphasizes shared success, collective responsibility, and mutual trust. It is no longer about two sides making a deal; it is about telling The Story of Us.

Bridge-Building Behaviors

Behaviors at this level are firmly at COLLABORATING. The leader has moved from ISOLATING toward COLLABORATING and has built a culture where collaboration is the default state of how the business runs. Different groups do not just talk; they actively collaborate on projects and strategic moves as part of their routine. The leader has built a culture where silos have mostly disappeared. In this environment, bridge-building is no longer a specific "activity" the leader has to plan; it is the natural state of how the business runs. Teams fluidly support each other to reach shared goals.

The Language Building Zone

At Level 6, the leader has closed much of the gap in the Language Building Zone. The gap between words and actions has mostly closed because collaboration is "embedded" in the culture. The leader's language and their actions now back each other up very well. However, the leader's job in this zone shifts from building to inspiration. They no longer need to tear down walls; instead, they use language to keep the collective energy high so the team does not drift back toward isolation.

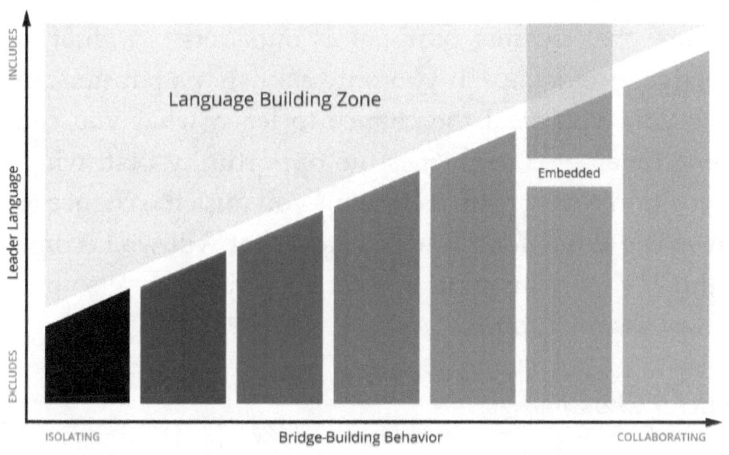

Level 6: Embedded (The Collaborative Leader)

The Lesson: The Story We Tell

Iris's story shows that when collaboration is embedded, the question of "who owns what" stops being relevant.

The Home Team Trap

Even after years of success, Iris saw her team start to treat a new acquisition (Firelight) as "them." They wanted to "assimilate" the new team rather than evolve with them. When Firelight joined, the default reflex was to teach them the Barkdale way; this meant absorbing, rather than co-authoring. The trap is assuming that a strong culture means a fixed culture. At Level 6, the leader treats new groups as partners who will change the culture, not as outsiders who must conform to it.

The Silent Thief

Iris knew that treating partners as outsiders is a thief of Collective Intelligence. If you only ask what a partner can do for you, you steal the chance to learn what you can become together. The thief is the opportunity cost: when you position a new team as "them," you miss the chance to evolve. The Embedded leader asks "what will we become together?" so that integration is a two-way exchange, not a one-way assimilation.

The Echo Chamber

The "Story Circle" ritual proved that when people share their struggles as a collective narrative, the boundaries between Documentary and Live Events disappear into "our project." The echo chamber at Level 6 is the opposite of siloed thinking, it is the repeated reinforcement of "we" until it becomes the only story people know how to tell.

The Pivot: Changing the Script

The pivot here shows how Iris used Bridge-Building language to stop the "us vs. them" mindset before it could take root during the acquisition.

The Script Shift

Iris moved the focus from protection to evolution by changing how the leadership team viewed new arrivals:

"Instead of asking 'how do we integrate Firelight into our way of working,' I want us to ask 'what will our way of working become once Firelight is part of us?' We are not here to train them to be like us; we are here to co-author a new chapter of who we are together."

Reviewing the Embedded Level

A leader at the Embedded level has achieved a rare state of harmony but must fight against complacency. Look for these performance "leaks":

The "Good Partner" Praise

Saying "another team was a great partner," which subtly implies they are still an external entity rather than part of the whole. When you praise a team as a "great partner," you are still drawing a line between "us" and "them." The Embedded leader describes the win as "we delivered" or "our team", so that the other group is not linguistically set apart. Partner praise is a leak that reintroduces the boundary just when you thought it was gone.

The "Extra Mile" Frame

Describing a standard collaborative task as "going above and beyond," which implies that staying in a silo is the normal track. When you frame collaboration as exceptional, you imply that the default is non-collaboration. The Embedded leader treats cross-functional work as the baseline: "that's how we operate." The extra-mile frame is a leak because it rewards behavior that should already be the norm. In doing so, it suggests the norm is something else.

Legacy Labeling

Using "Old Northstar" vs. "New Firelight" talk, which creates a hierarchy instead of a synthesis. When you label groups by their origin, you preserve the mental model of separate tribes. The Embedded leader uses one identity: "the way we work," "our culture," "our team." Legacy labeling is a leak that keeps the integration incomplete in people's minds.

The "Guest" Distinction

Welcoming a leader from another division as a "visitor" rather than as a co-owner of the space. Once you call someone a guest, you have drawn a boundary. The Embedded leader introduces everyone as a colleague or co-owner. The guest distinction is a small linguistic leak that says "this is our space, and you are in it" instead of "this is our space, and you are a part of it."

Lopsided Celebrations

Hosting a success dinner where the invite list is mostly the Home Team with only a few "guests" from the partner group. The composition of the celebration sends a message. When one team dominates the room, the story being told is "we did it, with some help." The Embedded leader ensures that celebrations reflect the collective: mixed tables, shared credit, one guest list that looks like the actual team.

How Iris Levels Up

To move to the Seamless level, Iris must move from mastery to artistry. She must set a "gold standard" where collaboration feels like the only natural state.

Listen for this Language

The "Effort" Correction

When someone is praised for "breaking down silos," correct the focus to the outcome (like Speed-to-Market) to signal that collaboration is the baseline, not a bonus. When you celebrate the act of breaking down silos, you imply that silos are still the norm and that collaboration is special. The Embedded leader redirects praise to the outcome: "We hit the launch date because we worked as one team." The effort correction teaches the organization that collaboration is expected, not heroic.

Identity Erase

In presentations, remove all functional team names and attribute success only to cross-functional project names. When you say "Documentary and Streaming delivered," you have named two teams. When you say "Project Aurora delivered," you have named one outcome. Identity erase is a linguistic discipline that makes the collective the default unit of attribution.

The "New Normal" Vocabulary

Strictly forbid the word "onboarding" for new groups; use "evolution" or "co-authoring." "Onboarding" implies that the new group is being fitted into an existing mold."Evolution" or "co-authoring" implies that the whole is changing. The vocabulary shift signals that integration is mutual, not one-way.

Future-State We

Describe future risks as threats to "our shared ecosystem" rather than to one department's KPI. When you talk about risk in terms of "our ecosystem," you keep the collective frame. When you talk about "Marketing's pipeline" or "Engineering's backlog," you have slipped back into silo language. A "Future-state We" keeps a shared horizon.

The "No-Label" Intro

Introduce a colleague simply as "my colleague" without mentioning their functional title or department. When you say "This is Sam from Engineering," you have labeled. When you say "This is Sam, my colleague," you have left the label out. The no-label intro is a small habit that reinforces the idea that function is secondary to the quality of the relationship.

Behaviors to Observe

The "Story Circle" Ritual

Create a regular, agenda-free forum for sharing stories about how work happened, not just status reports on what happened. The Story Circle is not a status meeting. It is a ritual where the only currency is narrative, and the only rule is that the narrative is collective. The ritual is a behavioral anchor for Level 6.

The "Shadow" Mandate

Require all leaders to complete a one-week "Shadow Rotation" inside a partner department before being promoted. The shadow mandate ensures that no one advances without having lived inside another team's context. It is a structural commitment that leadership is cross-functional by requirement, not by choice.

The "Mixed" Interview

Give a peer from a partner function the power to veto your new hires. When a partner can block a hire, you are saying that fit with the ecosystem matters as much as fit with your team. The mixed interview is a high-trust behavior that makes the collective the gatekeeper.

Decentralized Resolution

When a conflict is brought to you, send it back to the mixed team and tell them to return only when they have a shared proposal. Decentralized resolution is a behavioral commitment that the leader will not be the silo-busting hero; the team will.

The "Shared Wallet"

Create a budget that can only be unlocked by a joint signature from two different functional leads. When money requires two signatures from two functions, you have made collaboration structural. The shared wallet is a tangible signal that resources transparently flow across boundaries by design.

How to Avoid Sliding Back

Complacency is the enemy of Level 6 success. The leader must keep the energy of the collective alive.

Listen for this Language

Possessive Reversion

Reverting to "My P&L" or "My Headcount" during a moment of high budget pressure. Under stress, the old language returns."My" reasserts ownership and boundaries. The Embedded leader catches the slip and reframes: "our P&L," "our capacity," "our headcount." Possessive reversion is an early warning that the leader is under pressure and a signal they may be retreating toward silo thinking.

The Identity Gap

Letting the words "us" and "them" creep back into routine updates about a new team. When you talk about a new acquisition or a new department as "them," you have reopened the boundary. The Embedded leader uses "we" from day one, even before the integration is complete, so that the language leads the reality.

The "DNA" Fallacy

Claiming "Collaboration is in our DNA now" to justify stopping active training or cultural rituals. When you say it is in the DNA, you imply that the work is done. Culture is not DNA; it is habit. Habits require reinforcement. The Embedded leader keeps the rituals and the language work going because complacency is the biggest risk at Level 6.

Efficiency Justifications

Proposing to skip joint sessions because "we are already aligned." When you skip the ritual in the name of efficiency, you are betting that alignment will hold without reinforcement. The Embedded leader protects the recurring forums, such as Story Circles and joint reviews, because they are the maintenance that keeps the culture from drifting.

Task Force Labeling

This is calling a project a "Cross-Functional Task Force," which implies that normal work is not cross-functional. When you label something as "cross-functional," you imply that the default is single-function. The Embedded leader avoids the label; the work is just "the project" or "the initiative," and the cross-functional nature is an assumed default.

Behavioral Risks

Ritual Erosion

Shortening or canceling the "Story Circle" in favor of tactical syncs. When the ritual gets cut for "more important" meetings, the message is that the culture work is optional. The Embedded leader protects the ritual. Ritual erosion is a behavioral leak that often starts with one cancellation and becomes a pattern.

The Crisis Retreat

Calling a closed-door meeting of only your functional direct reports during a sudden emergency. In a crisis, the reflex is to huddle with "your" team. The crisis retreat is the behavioral equivalent of possessive language: we have our war room, they have theirs. The Embedded leader either includes the partner team in the crisis response or explicitly hands off to a joint structure so that the crisis does not become a silo moment.

Process Bifurcation

Allowing a sub-team to create a "shadow process" because the shared workflow feels too slow. When one team builds a workaround that bypasses the shared process, they have reintroduced a boundary. The Embedded leader surfaces and dismantles shadow processes so that the one-way-of-working stays real.

Vertical Onboarding

Training a new hire using only materials from their specific vertical, ignoring the broader context. When onboarding is vertical-only, the new hire inherits the old mental model. The Embedded leader ensures that every new hire learns the collective story: how the teams work together, what "we" means, and why boundaries are soft.

Micro-Friction Neglect

Choosing to ignore a small inter-team conflict because "it's not a big deal." Small frictions, left unaddressed, compound. The Embedded leader treats micro-frictions as early warnings. Naming and addressing them before they grow is how the culture stays healthy when the spotlight is off.

Level 7: Seamless (The Harmonized Leader)

Executive Summary

The "Seamless" leader eliminates the "Entropy Tax." This hidden tax is the subtle, silent cost of organizational drift. By maintaining the bridge network, they ensure that high-performance collaboration remains the path of least resistance, preventing the expensive slide back into silos.

Strategic Concepts

1. ***Seamless ≠ Effortless:** A frictionless organization looks easy from the outside, but it is the result of rigorous, daily maintenance. The moment the inspections stop, the old walls start rebuilding themselves.*
2. ***Patrol Over Construction:** The leader's role shifts from building bridges to protecting them. The primary task is now vigilance against complacency.*
3. ***Micro-Friction is a Signal:** In a seamless environment, even small hesitations or "us vs. them" jokes are treated as early warning signs of regression, not trivial annoyances.*
4. ***Identity Fusion:** The concept of "functional territory" disappears. Success is never attributed to a department (e.g., "Sales won"); it is attributed only to the collective value stream.*
5. ***The Gold Standard:** The Seamless team serves as the "teaching mode" for the rest of the company, exporting culture and talent to the less mature.*

Tactical Actions

1. ***The "Effort" Correction**: If someone is praised for "breaking down silos," interrupt to correct the focus. Praise the outcome (Speed), not the expectation (Collaboration).*
2. ***Identity Erasure**: Remove all functional team names (e.g., "Marketing," "Engineering") from internal "Win" slides. Attribute success solely to cross-functional project names.*
3. ***The "No-Label" Intro**: Introduce colleagues to external partners without using their functional titles. (e.g., "This is my partner, Sarah," not "This is Sarah from Legal").*
4. ***The Maintenance Defense**: Explicitly protect the budget for "soft" rituals (like joint offsites). When finance asks to cut them for "efficiency," defend them as critical infrastructure.*
5. ***The "New Kid" Clock**: Set a strict expiration date (e.g., 7 days) on referring to a new team or acquisition as "Them." After one week, they are "Us," with no exceptions.*

The Bridge Watch

Background

The question other executives often asked Josephine Alvarez was some variation of the same thing. How did you do it? The questions came from other divisions, from competitor companies, from business schools writing case studies about her division. They all wanted to know the secret behind what the Commercial division had become under her leadership.

Jo always gave the same answer, and it always seemed to disappoint them.

"There is no trick. There is no moment when you flip a switch and declare victory. It is years of work, followed by more years of work. And the work never stops."

They wanted a formula. What Jo offered instead was a philosophy. The highest form of collaboration was not a destination but a discipline. Seamless collaboration was not a state to be achieved but a bridge to be maintained. As soon as you stopped paying attention, everything began to unravel.

The Invisible Boundaries

On a Wednesday morning, Jo walked through the open workspace that housed what had once been four separate departments: Sales, Account Management, Customer Success, and Revenue Operations. The organizational chart still reflected those distinctions, but the physical space told a different story.

There were no walls. No department-specific areas. Teams clustered by project, by account, by initiative. No one had orchestrated this arrangement. No one needed to.

A junior account manager, new to the company, approached Jo at the coffee station.

"Can I ask you something? I came from a company where Sales and Customer Success basically hated each other. Here, I cannot even tell where one team ends and another begins. What makes this place different?"

"There are a lot of things. But mostly, it is how we talk. Over time, the way we describe what we are doing shapes what we actually do. If you talk about 'your team' and 'their team,' you start to believe that a boundary exists. If you talk about 'our work' and 'our customers,' the boundary disappears."

"So it is just language?"

"Language is never 'just' anything. Language is how we construct reality. When people here say 'we,' they mean all of us. That is not an accident. That is years of deliberate construction."

"And it keeps working?"

"It keeps working because we keep working at it. The moment we assume it is permanent is the moment it starts to fade."

The Stress Test

That afternoon, Jo received an email from one of her most trusted directors.

Hey Jo. I have been thinking about our Quarterly Business Reviews. We have been doing cross-functional QBRs for almost five years now. But I am wondering if we have outgrown the format. We are so aligned now that the joint prep sessions feel redundant. I think we could streamline by having each team present independently.

Jo read the email twice. On the surface, it was a reasonable efficiency suggestion. But something about it kept nagging at her.

She picked up the phone.

"Can we talk through your email?"

"Of course. The prep for joint sessions is substantial. If we could do our piece independently, we would save eight to ten hours per quarter."

"I hear that. But what do those joint prep sessions actually accomplish?"

"They keep everyone on the same page. They make sure we are telling a consistent story."

"Right. And what happens if we stop doing them?"

"Probably nothing, at first. We are so aligned we would stay consistent anyway."

"At first," Jo repeated."That is the key phrase. What about after a year? Two years?"

The line was quiet.

"What you are describing is a symptom of our success," Jo continued gently."The collaboration feels so natural that the work required to maintain it feels unnecessary. But the work is not unnecessary. It is invisible. The reason we are aligned is because we keep doing the things that align us. If we stop, then the alignment will drift. Slowly at first, then faster."

"I was hoping we had reached a point where we did not have to work so hard at it."

"That point does not exist. It is a mirage. The bridge holds because we keep running the inspections. Skip them, and the first crack you notice will be the one that is already too wide to patch."

The Bridge at Scale

Every year, Jo hosted the "Seamless Summit," where the entire division reflected on how they worked, not just what they achieved.

Midway through the afternoon, Jo took the stage.

"I want to talk about the word 'seamless.' We use it to describe what we have built here. And on the best days, that is what it feels like. Work flows across boundaries without friction. People help each other without being asked. The distinction between 'my job' and 'your job' disappears into 'our job.'"

She paused.

"But I want to be careful about what 'seamless' means. It does not mean effortless. It does not mean automatic. And it definitely does not mean permanent."

She clicked a slide showing a massive suspension bridge under inspection, workers on the cables at dawn.

"This is what seamless collaboration looks like to me. A bridge that carries heavy traffic because someone inspects the cables every morning. Tightening, reinforcing, clearing debris from the deck. The reliability you see is the product of work you do not see. The moment that maintenance stops, the structure begins to weaken."

She looked directly at the audience.

"So do not take this for granted. Every day, make the choice to patrol the span. Use words that unite. Take actions that connect. The secret is not complicated. It is just vigilance. Every day, every interaction, every word. That is the work. And it never ends."

Breaking It Down

The Home Team's Language

At this final stage, the leader's language is unmatched in its clarity. Your words do not just convince people to work together; they describe a shared world where collaboration is the natural path. This communication is instinctive and consistent. It acts as a stabilizing force that stops old labels or exclusions from coming back.

Bridge-Building Behaviors

Behaviors at the Seamless level are fluid and frictionless. On the Bridge-Building axis, you have moved all the way from ISOLATING to firmly at COLLABORATING; collaboration is no longer an initiative, it is simply how the system runs. On the Leader Language axis, your language lives in INCLUDES, reinforcing a shared identity instead of separate territories. The organization chart might still show different departments, but there is effectively zero operational friction between them in day-to-day work. You actively guard against slipping back to ISOLATING or EXCLUDES.

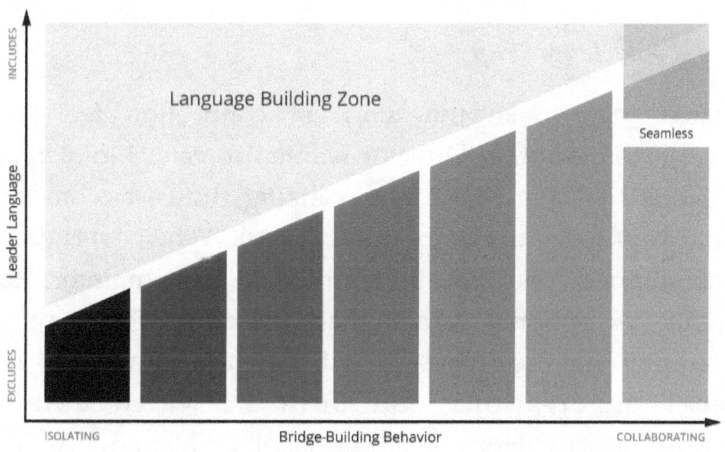

Level 7: Seamless (The Harmonized Leader)

The Language Building Zone

Level 7 marks the apex of the Language Building Zone, but it is also the zone of highest risk. Because everything feels so easy, it is tempting to become lazy and assume the culture will maintain itself. The asymmetry is gone, and your words and actions match perfectly, but you must stay vigilant. The work here is stewardship. You must intercept any exclusionary talk before it reopens old divides, to protect the spans you have built.

The Lesson: The Bridge Watch

Jo's story shows that the highest form of collaboration is a discipline, not a destination.

The Home Team Trap

Success can make the work of connection feel like "overhead". Another Director wanted to cancel joint prep sessions to "save time," not realizing those sessions are what kept the walls from growing back. When everything feels aligned, you may be tempted to treat maintenance rituals as optional rather than essential. The trap is assuming that the ecosystem will stay healthy without the very conversations that built it, which quietly reintroduces the Home Team vs. Another Team divide.

The Silent Thief

Jo understood that "efficiency" is often a thief of Friction Reduction. When you cut the meetings, rituals, or shared prep that keep people aligned, you create space for misalignment to grow, even if you temporarily gain calendar time. The thief here is not a dramatic blow-up but the slow erosion of shared understanding and trust. By the time you notice, the cost in rework and friction is far higher than the "efficiency" savings you thought you had gained.

The Echo Chamber

Even a junior manager noticed that people "just help each other". This happens because Jo refused to let a new leader draw lines or "protect turf" during his first week, interrupting any language that would separate groups. When you enforce a consistent "we" story, the organization begins to echo that language back to you in its habits. The echo chamber at Seamless is the positive reinforcement loop where inclusive language and collaborative behavior keep amplifying each other.

The Pivot: Changing the Script

The pivot here shows how Jo used Bridge-Building language to stop the return of silos before they could take root. When a manager used "they" to describe a new team, Jo corrected it immediately.

The Script Shift

Jo used the Story of Us to maintain the company's Collective Intelligence:

"Derek, you just drew a line by saying 'their' opportunities. That framing creates a boundary we don't need. Try calling them 'the leads we are developing together. ' It might feel awkward, but it changes how you think. And how you think determines what is possible for this company."

Reviewing the Seamless Level

A leader at the Seamless level must act as a steward. Look for these structural cracks that signal a risk of regression:

The "Autopilot" Assumption

Believing the culture is "in our DNA" and no longer requires active maintenance. When you start telling yourself the system will run on its own, you stop doing the small, deliberate things that keep it healthy. This assumption is dangerous because it hides behind pride in what you have built. The moment you think the work is finished, old walls start going up again, brick-by-brick.

Efficiency Justifications

Proposing to cancel joint rituals or prep sessions to "free up capacity". On paper, cutting a recurring forum may look like a smart use of time, especially when everyone feels aligned. In practice, those rituals are often the only places where cross-functional understanding is refreshed and reinforced. When you justify cuts in the name of efficiency, you are usually trading short-term time savings for long-term friction and confusion.

Maintenance as Overhead

This is viewing relationship-building as a distraction from "real work". At Seamless, the relationships are the infrastructure that makes the real work possible. When you mentally categorize check-ins, shared reviews, or informal touch-points as "extra," you are already devaluing the system that keeps silos from returning. Treat maintenance as core work, not as nice-to-have, or it will be one of the first things sacrificed under pressure.

Micro-Friction Neglect

Ignoring small inter-team conflicts because they seem "low-stakes". A sarcastic comment, a missed invitation, or a minor scheduling slight can look trivial in isolation. But at this level, micro-frictions are early indicators that old identity lines are reappearing. When you address them quickly and directly, you reinforce the norms; when you let them slide, you silently grant permission for bigger conflicts to begin forming.

The "New Kid" Labeling

Letting "Them" or "The New Guys" labels last beyond the first week of an integration. The words may sound harmless, even affectionate, but they preserve a mental boundary between "us" and "them." If you allow that language to persist, you cement the idea that new groups are visitors rather than co-owners. Your job is to shorten the time to "us" so that everyone hears and uses one shared identity as quickly as possible.

How Jo Stays Seamless

Maintenance at Level 7 requires constant, quiet action. Execute these Imperative Commands to keep patrolling the bridge network:

Listen for this Language

The "Effort" Correction

If someone is praised for "breaking down silos," direct them to focus on the business outcome, like Speed-to-Market. When you celebrate the heroic effort instead of the result, you imply that silos are the norm and collaboration is exceptional. By shifting the praise to the outcome, you teach people that working as one system is the baseline expectation. Over time, this correction helps the organization stop romanticizing firefights and start valuing seamless flow.

The Identity Erase

Remove all functional team names from "Wins" slides; attribute success only to the cross-functional project name. When you list Marketing, Sales, and Ops separately, you subtly reinforce that each group has its own victory. By naming only the shared initiative, you invite everyone to see themselves as part of that single story. This small act of editing slides is a powerful signal that the unit of success is the ecosystem, and it avoids silo hardening.

The "New Normal" Vocabulary

Replace "onboarding" with "evolution," asking how "we" will change once a new team is here."Onboarding" suggests that the new group is fitting into an existing mold you control."Evolution" suggests that the whole will be reshaped by what they bring. When you change the words you use, you change how people think about integration: not as training outsiders to conform, but as a shared redesign of who you are together.

Future-State We

Describe future risks as threats to "our shared ecosystem" rather than to one department's budget. When you frame risk as "Marketing's pipeline" or "Engineering's backlog," you push people back into defending their own lane. By talking about "our ecosystem" and "our ability to serve customers," you keep everyone looking at the same horizon. This habit keeps planning conversations anchored in the whole, so trade-offs feel like shared design choices instead of zero-sum battles.

The "No-Label" Intro

Introduce colleagues from other functions as "my colleague" or "a leader on our team" without explicitly mentioning their department. The way you introduce people teaches others how to see them. When you lead with function, you lead with difference; when you lead with relationship, you lead with connection. Over time, the no-label intro helps dissolve the reflex to sort people by silo before you see them as partners.

Behaviors to Observe

The "Story Circle" Ritual

Keep a regular, agenda-free forum for sharing stories about how the work happened. When you make space for people to tell "we" stories, you reinforce the idea that success is co-created, not handed off between groups. These gatherings are not status meetings; they are narrative maintenance. The more often people practice telling the story of "us," the harder it becomes for old us-versus-them stories to take root again.

The "Shadow" Mandate

Ensure no leader is promoted without completing a rotation inside a partner department. When you require leaders to live inside another team's world, you make empathy and system thinking non-negotiable. This mandate turns cross-functional understanding from a nice bonus into a promotion gate. Over time, your leadership bench is filled with people who instinctively think in terms of the whole system rather than their own silo.

The "Mixed" Interview

Give a peer from a partner function the power to veto your new hires. When someone outside your line can stop a hire, it signals that fit with the ecosystem matters as much as fit with your own team. This practice forces candidates to demonstrate that they can operate across boundaries, not just down a narrow lane. It also reminds your existing leaders that they are accountable to the whole, not just to their own headcount plan.

Decentralized Resolution

Refuse to "break the tie" for a mixed team; tell them to stay in the room until they have one shared proposal. When you stop playing referee, you push responsibility for integration back to the people closest to the work. This slows decisions down in the moment but speeds them up over the long run by building the muscles for joint problem-solving. Every time you send a conflict back to the team, you reinforce that collaboration is not optional or escalated, but it is standard operating procedure.

The "Shared Wallet"

Maintain at least one budget line that requires a joint signature from two different functional leads to unlock. Money is one of the clearest signals of what an organization truly values. When you design a budget that cannot move without cross-functional agreement, you hard-wire collaboration into resource allocation. The shared wallet keeps both leaders accountable to the same outcomes, making it harder for any one silo to hoard resources at the expense of the whole.

Conclusion

The Ongoing Work

You have now walked the entire path of the BRIDGES Model. You started with Diane Kowalski's fortress walls and ended with Jo Alvarez's unbroken spans. Along the way, you met leaders in crisis, leaders in transition, and leaders who mastered the art of dissolving the boundaries that divide organizations.

If this book has done its job, you understand something crucial. The path has no end.

The BRIDGES Model is not a ladder to be climbed and conquered. It is a discipline to be practiced. A bridge to be maintained. A conversation to be renewed every day. The moment a leader believes they have "arrived" at seamless collaboration is the precise moment the old walls begin rebuilding themselves.

The Journey: From Fear to Stewardship

Leaders who move through this model undergo similar transformations. At its core, the BRIDGES Model traces a journey from fear to confidence. From the defensive isolation of the blocked leader to the quiet assurance of the harmonized steward.

Consider where we began. Diane Kowalski installed a badge reader at her department entrance. She moved meetings to times when outsiders could not attend. She told her team to "go dark." These were not the actions of a bad leader. They were the actions of a frightened one.

The fear that drives blocked leaders is primal. It is the fear of losing what has been built. The fear of being misunderstood by those who do not appreciate the complexity of the work. The fear that opening the door will somehow diminish what makes the team special.

But walls built for protection become prisons. Diane's fortress did not protect her team. It trapped them.

The journey from Blocked to Seamless is marked by a gradual softening of the boundaries that define who is "us" and who is "them." Nathan Okafor began by simply attending meetings he had previously skipped. Samira Okonkwo launched her "cartography project" to understand departments she had been ignoring. Vanessa Reyes declared that her team and another group were "one unit now." Each step represented a willingness to expand the definition of "we."

At the highest levels, the relationship with other groups transforms completely. Iris Delgado no longer thinks about collaboration as something to be achieved. It is simply how work happens.

Jo Alvarez walks through her workspace watching teams cluster naturally around problems, and she cannot remember when this became normal. The insight here is that a truly Seamless leader knows it is not permanent.

Jo's response reveals the mindset of the steward: "The bridge holds because we keep running the inspections. Skip them, and the first crack you notice will be the one that is already too wide to patch."

The narrative arc of the BRIDGES Model is not a hero's journey with a triumphant conclusion. It is a story of ongoing commitment. Of choosing every day to do the work that keeps the boundaries soft, the silos from hardening, and the bridges strong.

The Hidden Lesson: Language Builds Reality

Beneath the frameworks and checklists, there is a deeper lesson. Leaders are not primarily managers of tasks. They are managers of identity.

Every time you speak or act, you signal to your team who is "us" and who is "them." You are either hardening the boundary or softening it. Either expanding the definition of "we" or contracting it.

This is why language is so central to the model. Words are not just communication. They are construction. When Diane told her team "We are going dark," she was not merely giving an instruction. She was constructing a reality in which the outside world was a threat. When Evelyn Matsuda asked her team to notice whether their language "includes or excludes," she was training them to become conscious architects of their own shared identity.

The model traces an evolution in leadership language:

- ***At Level 1-2****, language is defensive. It draws boundaries and assigns blame. You hear stories about "them" and "their process" and "what they do to us." The leader's words reinforce the idea that the Home Team must be protected from everyone else.*
- ***At Level 3-4****, language becomes deliberate. It consciously bridges gaps and validates other perspectives. You begin to hear questions instead of accusations and invitations instead of ultimatums. The leader is learning to open the gate and experiment with new ways of saying "we."*
- ***At Level 5-6****, language becomes inspirational. It creates and sustains shared reality. The leader speaks in a way that sounds the same to every audience, aligning Home Team and partner teams around a single story. Their words no longer just fix problems; they maintain a shared purpose.*
- ***At Level 7****, language becomes stewardship. The leader's words serve primarily to maintain what has been built, catching small slips toward EXCLUDES before they harden into new silos. This work is less about building bridges and more about patrolling them.*

This progression reveals the hidden lesson. Leadership is fundamentally about the words we choose. Not as decoration on top of "real" actions, but as the primary way we build reality.

Final Verdict: The Bridge Builder's Work

We return, at the end, to the metaphor that runs through the title of this book. Silos and the bridges to defeat them.

Jo Alvarez understood something that the executives who came to study her division never quite grasped. There is no secret. There is no methodology that sustains itself simply because it is implemented. There is no framework that requires no further attention once understood. There is only the work. Daily, unglamorous, and often invisible. The work of maintaining what has been built.

The bridge metaphor captures several essential truths:

Bridges require site work.

Before anything can span a divide, the ground on both sides must be surveyed and prepared. At the lower levels of the model, your work is primarily preparatory; using language to signal safety, taking small actions to crack open the black box, and beginning to dismantle the walls that kept other teams out.

These early moves may not look dramatic from the outside, but they are how you establish the footings so the first span can hold weight.

Bridges require active engineering.

Spans do not assemble themselves. At the middle levels, you are actively building: investigating how other groups work, deciding to commit to partnership, and grounding the relationship in shared reality. You are not just opening the gate; you are laying cable, setting deck plates, and load-testing every connection against the old reflexes of "us versus them."

Bridges are always under stress.

Corrosion never sleeps. The regression watchlists throughout this book are catalogs of structural threats. These are the small phrases, the minor retreats, the "efficiency" shortcuts that seem harmless but slowly weaken what has been constructed. When you ignore those signals, you allow the old silo walls to reassemble in the space you fought hard to clear. When you catch them early, you keep the spans open and the traffic flowing.

A strong bridge makes the engineering invisible.

This is the paradox of the Seamless level. When collaboration flows effortlessly, observers assume it happened naturally. They see the smooth traffic but not the hours spent inspecting cables, reinforcing joints, and clearing debris from the deck.

In organizations, the more effectively you reduce friction, the more people will believe "this is just how it is here" and forget the intentional work that made it so. Your job is to remember, and to keep doing the quiet maintenance even when no one is applauding.

The bridge builder's work never ends.

There is no final inspection after which the bridge can be left alone. At Level 7, you have not finished building bridges; you have accepted that bridge-building is now your permanent vocation. The moment you stop listening for boundary-hardening language, watching for micro-frictions, or reinforcing the Story of Us, the cracks begin to widen. Stewardship is not a phase of leadership; it is the ongoing work of leadership itself.

The Choice Before You

Now you have read the stories and you have absorbed the frameworks. You have examined the protocols and the watchlists. Now comes the only question that matters.

What will you do tomorrow?

The BRIDGES Model cannot transform you. It can only illuminate the path. The actual work belongs to you.

But here is the promise that underlies everything in this book. The work is worth it.

Organizations that operate as collections of warring silos are not just inefficient. They are miserable. People spend their energy defending territory instead of creating value. They leave work exhausted not from meaningful effort but from pointless friction.

Organizations where bridges have been built are qualitatively different places to work. Problems get solved because the right people can find each other. Information flows because the walls are not there to stop it. People experience the deep satisfaction of genuine collaboration, and they feel a sense of being part of something larger than their immediate team.

You have the power to create that kind of organization. Not instantly. Not easily. But definitively. The seven levels of the BRIDGES Model serve as maps drawn by leaders who have made the journey. The path exists. Others have walked it. Will you?

What Story Are We Telling Today?

Every day, you are telling a story to your team. Through your words and your actions. Through what you celebrate and what you challenge. Through who you include and who you exclude. You are constructing a narrative about what matters, who belongs, and what is possible.

The question is not whether you will tell a story. The question is: what story will you tell?

Will it be a story of walls and territories, of "us" and "them," of protection, isolation, and another chapter in the long history of organizational silos?

Or will it be a story of bridges and open lanes, of "we" and "together," of connection and stewardship? A story in which you choose, again and again, to keep the spans strong and the paths clear.

The choice is yours. The work begins tomorrow.

Build your BRIDGES. And never stop walking them.

Appendix

Practical Tools to Help You Grow Connections Between Groups in Your Organization

The Leader's Discussion Guide

This is your guide to maturing intergroup leadership in your organization using the BRIDGES Model.

As a sponsor, you are the catalyst for transforming how your organization collaborates. The BRIDGES Model provides a diagnostic framework and practical language for moving teams from territorial isolation to collaborative stewardship. This guide equips you to lead meaningful discussions that translate the book's concepts into organizational action.

The premise is simple but profound: smart people do not automatically collaborate. Bridge-building between groups requires direct effort, specific language patterns, and consistent maintenance. Your sponsorship signals that this work matters.

How to Use This Guide

This guide is organized into four sections:

- **Foundation Discussions**: Core concepts to establish with your leadership team
- **Level-by-Level Dialogues**: Discussion questions for each of the BRIDGES levels
- **Diagnostic Exercises**: Team activities to surface friction points
- **Implementation Actions**: Concrete next steps for you to take with your organization

Recommended approach

Begin with the Foundation Discussions in your first session. In subsequent meetings, work through the Level-by-Level Dialogues that correspond to where your teams currently operate. Use the Diagnostic Exercises to create shared awareness, then move to Implementation Actions.

Facilitation Notes

Guidance for effective discussions using this guide.

Setting the Right Tone

- Frame this as development, not criticism. The goal is growth, not assigning blame.
- Acknowledge that silo behavior is natural and it stems from our biological wiring for in-group protection. The work is about overriding instincts, not fixing character flaws.
- Model vulnerability by sharing your own friction points first.
- Emphasize that the BRIDGES model is descriptive, not prescriptive and it helps diagnose the current state and chart a path forward.

Common Resistance Patterns

"We don't have time for this."

Redirect: Calculate the friction tax. How much time is lost to rework, delayed decisions, and workarounds? The time invested in bridge-building saves execution speed.

"Other teams are the problem."

Redirect: This is exactly the "Home Team Trap." The model asks us to focus on our language and behavior because those are the things we control.

"We're already collaborating."

Redirect: Use the 14-Point Inspection. Collaboration is often assumed but not practiced. The diagnostic reveals gaps between perception and reality.

"This is too soft."

Redirect: The model's outcomes are hard: speed-to-market, margin, capacity. Language is the tool; business performance is the result.

Sustaining Momentum

- **Schedule recurring discussions:** monthly at minimum during active development.
- **Track progress** through the 14-Point Inspection quarterly.
- **Celebrate movement between levels:** even small shifts matter.
- **Remember Jo's lesson:** "The moment we stop paying attention is the moment everything begins to unravel."
- **Maintain stewardship:** this is ongoing gardening work, not a one-time construction project.

Final Thought: Bridges between intergroup leaders need continuous attention. Your role as sponsor is not to declare victory but to model vigilance. Every day, every interaction, every word because that is the work. It will always continue, so embrace the journey. Start building your bridges.

For more resources like these, please visit the book's website. Go to: thesilobook.com/

Part One: Foundation Discussions

Before diving into specific levels, establish a shared understanding of the model's core concepts with your leadership team.

The Language Building Zone

Key Concept: At lower maturity levels, a leader must talk their way into trust before they can act their way into partnership. Language carries disproportionate weight when trust is low.

Discussion Questions:

1. When you hear how leaders in your organization talk about other departments, what patterns do you notice? Is the language constructive or defensive?
2. Think of a recent cross-functional initiative that struggled. How much of the friction was about process versus how people talked about each other?
3. Where in your organization do you see the gap between what leaders say ("We value collaboration") and what they actually do?

The Silent Thief

Key Concept: Friction between teams steals speed, margin, and morale without triggering a crisis alarm. This "Friction Tax" compounds over time, appearing in the business as missed deadlines, rework, slow decisions, and high turnover.

Discussion Questions:

1. If you had to estimate, what percentage of your organization's capacity is lost to friction between teams? Where do you see it most?
2. Can you name a specific decision in the last quarter that was delayed because teams couldn't align? What was the cost?
3. What "workarounds" have your teams developed to bypass other departments? What does this signal?

The Home Team Trap

Key Concept: Leaders naturally create in-groups ("The Home Team") for psychological safety. But unchecked loyalty to the Home Team leads to isolation, fortress behavior, and treating other departments as obstacles rather than partners.

Discussion Questions:

1. Which leaders in your organization have the strongest "fortress" mentality? What drives it? Protection, control, or something else?
2. How do you personally balance protecting your team with serving the broader organization?
3. When was the last time you heard someone say "That's their problem, not ours"? What happened as a result?

Part Two: Level-by-Level Dialogues

Use these discussions to explore each level of the BRIDGES Model. Focus on the levels where your organization operates now and the level immediately above as an aspiration.

Level 1: Blocked (The Isolated Leader)

Archetype Example	***The "Black Box" department. Operationally excellent but organizationally isolated.***
Behavior Example	*Creating hard boundaries by installing a badge reader to protect a team from physical access.*
Character Example	*Diane Kowalski at Vantage Retail Group (The Fortress on the Fourth Floor).*

Discussion Questions:

1. Diane believed she was "protecting her team from distraction." Where might similar logic be operating in our organization?
2. The $14 million inventory miss resulted from data sitting unused. What critical information might be "trapped" in our departments right now?
3. Which of our teams has earned a reputation as "impossible to work with"? What would change if we addressed this?
4. What is our current response time to cross-functional inquiries? Is there a "24-hour acknowledgment" standard we should adopt?

Level 2: Receptive (The Aware Leader)

Archetype Example	***Attends meetings, smiles in hallways, but creates "Politeness Tax" through passive non-participation.***
Behavior Example	*"Guest" mentality in meetings, bandwidth defense, inconsistent signaling, "us vs. them" in private.*
Character Example	*Nathan Okafor at Bellwether Financial ("The Door Left Ajar").*

Discussion Questions:

1. Nathan said "We want to help" but he then "deprioritized" the project. Where do we see similar gaps between stated intent and actual follow-through?
2. How often do our leaders attend cross-functional meetings as "guests" rather than co-owners of the outcome?
3. Nathan slipped back to "us vs. them" language under stress. How do our leaders speak differently in public versus private?
4. What would it take for each of our leaders to schedule a "discovery session" with a peer? Would thirty minutes solely to learn their goals, with no asks on the agenda be enough?

Level 3: Investigating (The Open Leader)

Archetype Example	***The "Cartographer" who maps partner teams' reality, eliminating the "Re-Work Tax."***
Behavior Example	*"Audit" perception, extractive learning without closing the loop, retreating at first pushback.*
Character Example	*Samira Okonkwo at Meridian Software ("The Cartographer").*

Discussion Questions:

1. Samira discovered that "ship" meant different things to different departments. What terminology in our organization might be causing similar confusion?
2. Roland felt Samira's questions were "extractive" until she started publishing "What Sales Taught Us" documents. How do we close the loop when we gather insights from other teams?
3. When did we last invite a partner team into an "ugly draft" stage of our planning, rather than only seeking sign-off on polished decisions?
4. Which of our leaders would benefit from sitting in on another team's internal review? Not to critique, but to understand their daily friction.

Level 4: Deciding (The Connected Leader)

Archetype Example	***The tipping point, or consciously choosing shared identity, eliminating the "Negotiation Tax."***
Behavior Example	*Transactional framing, possessive regression ("my budget"), escalation bypass, "despite" narrative.*
Character Example	*Vanessa Reyes at Coastal Dynamics ("The Line in the Sand").*

Discussion Questions:

1. Vanessa declared "we succeed together or fail together." What would a similar declaration look like for two departments we need to unite?
2. During the outage, both teams reached for blame. When crises hit our organization, do teams retreat to corners or mobilize as one unit?
3. Vanessa corrected "classic Infrastructure move" language in the break room. How do we address casual blame-language before it becomes toxic?
4. What is one "North Star" metric we could establish that requires two departments to succeed together for anyone to claim victory?

Level 5: Grounded (The Aligned Leader)

Archetype Example	***Stabilized partnership built on shared reality; teams move in lockstep, eliminating the "Alignment Tax."***
Behavior Example	*Laned success framing, polite deferral, "guest" dynamics, client/vendor framing of partnerships.*
Character Example	*Evelyn Matsuda at Castellex Therapeutics ("The Shared Ground")*

Discussion Questions:

1. Evelyn noticed her team naturally used "we" to describe both departments. Where do we already see this kind of language emerging organically?
2. When bad data emerged in the trial, Evelyn framed it as "science, not failure." How do we frame setbacks? Do we frame them as system issues or blame opportunities?
3. Evelyn said the work shifted from "construction to maintenance." Which partnerships have we built that now need tending rather than building?
4. Do we have any partnerships where leadership presents a "100% unified front" with no visible daylight? What would that take?

Level 6: Embedded (The Collaborative Leader)

Archetype Example	***Collaboration as default state; eliminates the "Integration Tax" when absorbing new teams.***
Behavior Example	*"Good partner" praise (implies external), "extra mile" framing, legacy labeling, ritual erosion.*
Character Example	*Iris Delgado at Barkdale Media Group ("The Story We Tell").*

Discussion Questions:

1. Iris's "Story Circle" required people to share achievements as collective narratives, never "my team did this." What ritual could we create that reinforces shared identity?
2. When Barkdale acquired Firelight, Iris asked "what will our way of working become?" rather than "how do we integrate them?" How do we approach integrations? Do we approach them as assimilation or evolution?
3. Iris adopted Firelight's "spark labs" practice across all divisions. What could we learn from teams we've recently absorbed rather than only teaching them?

Level 7: Seamless (The Harmonized Leader)

Archetype Example	***The gold standard. This is stewardship, not construction, and eliminates the "Entropy Tax" through constant vigilance.***
Behavior Example	*"Autopilot" assumption, efficiency justifications for cutting rituals, micro-friction neglect.*
Character Example	*Josephine Alvarez at the Commercial Division ("The Bridge Watch").*

Discussion Questions:

1. Jo told a director that cutting joint prep sessions would cause "slow drift, then faster." Where might we be tempted to cut collaborative rituals for efficiency?
2. Jo corrected Derek for drawing a line with "their" opportunities, saying "that framing creates a boundary we don't need." How quickly do we correct language slips?
3. "Seamless does not mean effortless." What does ongoing maintenance look like for our best partnerships? Are we actively tending or passively hoping?
4. If we have teams that have achieved seamless collaboration, how are we exporting their culture and practices to less mature parts of the organization?

Part Three: Diagnostic Exercises

These exercises help your leadership team surface friction points and create a shared awareness of where improvement is needed.

Exercise 1: The 14-Point Inspection

Purpose	***Individual self-assessment to establish baseline awareness***
Time Required	*~ 15 minutes individual* *~ 30 minutes group discussion*
Process	*Distribute copies of the 14-Point Inspection from the book. Have each leader complete it privately, then facilitate a discussion using these prompts:*

Discussion Questions:

1. Without revealing your score, what was the hardest question to answer honestly?
2. Which signal surprised you most when you realized you answered "yes"?
3. If we each improved on just one signal over the next quarter, which would have the greatest impact to the organization?

Audit Your Bridge Map: The 14-Point Inspection

This assessment checks for the specific "friction points" in the BRIDGES Model. Answer **YES** if the statement describes your current reality (even occasionally). Answer **NO** if it never happens.

Be honest with yourself. You cannot fix a crack you do not want to see.

#	*Signal*	*Yes*	*No*
1	Do you privately view other departments as obstacles to your goals rather than partners in them?	☐	☐
2	Is there a key peer in another department whose personal phone number is not saved in your contacts?	☐	☐
3	Do you attend cross-functional meetings but rarely volunteer to take on shared action items?	☐	☐
4	Do you smile and agree in joint meetings, only to complain to your own team immediately afterward?	☐	☐
5	When you ask another team for data, do they often get defensive or ask "why do you need this"?	☐	☐
6	Do you frequently use acronyms or team-specific jargon in mixed meetings without defining them?	☐	☐
7	In a crisis, is your first instinct to protect your team from blame rather than solving the shared problem?	☐	☐
8	Do you go to your manager to resolve conflicts with peers instead of working it out directly with them?	☐	☐
9	Do you use the word "handoff" or "transfer" to describe moving work between teams?	☐	☐
10	Do you maintain a separate roadmap or success metric that is not visible to your partner teams?	☐	☐
11	Do you thank partner leaders for "visiting" your meetings rather than treating them as co-owners of the space?	☐	☐
12	Do you hide budget surplus or talent capacity to ensure your team has a "safety buffer"?	☐	☐
13	Do you ignore small "us vs. them" jokes because they seem harmless or "just blowing off steam"?	☐	☐
14	Do you assume your team's collaborative culture is "permanent" and requires no active training or maintenance?	☐	☐

Scoring Your Self-Check

Count your total number of "YES" answers.

13–14 Friction Points: Level 1 — Blocked (The Isolated Leader)

- Diagnosis: Your team is operating in a deep silo. You are likely efficient internally, but invisible or a blocker to the rest of the organization."Us vs. Them" is the default operating model.
- Immediate Action: Focus on "Humanizing the Other Side." Schedule a coffee chat with one peer leader with no agenda other than to understand their current top three concerns.

11–12 Friction Points: Level 2 — Receptive (The Aware Leader)

- Diagnosis: You know friction exists and it bothers you, but you feel protecting your team is more important than fixing the system. You cooperate when forced, but collaborate rarely.
- Immediate Action: Focus on "low-stakes signaling." In your next cross-functional meeting, publicly validate a valid point made by a "rival" department.

9–10 Friction Points: Level 3 — Investigating (The Open Leader)

- Diagnosis: You are curious about better ways to work and have started building individual bridges, but your team's processes are still insular. You trade favors rather than sharing goals.
- Immediate Action: Focus on "shared vocabulary." Identify one acronym or term your team uses that confuses others, and officially redefine it in plain language for your partners.

7–8 Friction Points: Level 4 — Deciding (The Connected Leader)

- Diagnosis: You are actively trying to move from "me" to "we." You have good relationships with peers, but structural barriers (budget, metrics, tooling) still cause friction during crunch time.
- Immediate Action: Focus on "visible commitment." Volunteer your team to own a shared action item that benefits another department more than it benefits you right now.

5–6 Friction Points: Level 5 — Grounded (The Aligned Leader)

- Diagnosis: Alignment is becoming structural. You no longer view other departments as obstacles. Conflicts are resolved directly, but you still need to consciously maintain the connection.
- Immediate Action: Focus on "metric transparency." Share your team's internal success metrics with a partner team and ask them if those metrics help or hurt their goals.

3–4 Friction Points: Level 6 — Embedded (The Collaborative Leader)

- Diagnosis: Interdependence is the norm. Your team instinctively considers the "whole" before the "part." Hand-offs are rare; "hand-shakes" are common.
- Immediate Action: Focus on "joint resilience." In a crisis, skip the blame assignment and immediately convene a joint "swarm" team to solve the problem together.

0–2 Friction Points: Level 7 — Seamless (The Harmonized Leader)

- Diagnosis: You have dissolved the silo. Your leadership language turns friction into flow. You are not just running a team; you are tending to the organizational system.
- Immediate Action: Focus on "cultivation." Mentorship is your primary tool now. Identify a Level 3 leader and help them navigate their friction points.

Get the Full Data

This checklist tells you if you have friction.

To understand why, take the free digital assessment.

Visit: thesilobook.com

Exercise 2: The Language Audit

Purpose	***Individual self-assessment to establish baseline awareness***
Time Required	*~ 15 minutes individual* *~ 30 minutes group discussion*
Process	*Use a physical or digital whiteboard and draw a table with three columns. Use the two rows provided as examples to guide the conversation, and ask your team to share examples of destructive language and ideas for constructive alternatives.*

Destructive Language	***Where We Hear It***	***Constructive Alternative***
"That's a Sales problem."	*Product team stand-ups*	*"We have a customer impact issue"*
"They never respond."	*Executive meetings*	*"Our process has a gap at the handoff"*
(Add Your Examples)		

Debrief Questions:

1. Which destructive phrases appear most frequently across departments?
2. What would happen if we committed to using only the constructive alternatives for thirty days?

Exercise 3: The Friction Map

Purpose	***Identify the most costly friction points between teams and prioritize intervention.***
Time Required	*60 minutes*
Process	*Draw your organization's major functions as nodes on a whiteboard. For each connection between nodes, rate the friction level (1–5) and estimate the business cost. Focus discussion on the highest-cost connections.*

Discussion Questions:

1. Which two connections have the highest friction and highest business impact?
2. Where is friction historically high but currently improving? What changed?
3. If we could reduce friction by 50% in one connection, which would deliver the greatest ROI?
4. What level of the BRIDGES model describes each high-friction connection?

Exercise 4: Story Identification

Purpose	***Connect book scenarios to real organizational situations for deeper learning.***
Time Required	*45 minutes*
Process	*Have each leader identify which story character they recognize most in your organization.*

Discussion Questions:

1. Which story felt most familiar to our organization?
2. Do we have our own "Diane" (Blocked)? Do we have a "Nathan" (Receptive)? A "Samira" (Investigating)?
3. What "flashpoint" moment in the stories parallels something we've experienced?
4. If we wrote our own story for where we are today, what would the title be?

Part Four: Implementation Actions

Move from discussion to action with these sponsor-level commitments and organization-wide initiatives.

Sponsor Commitments

As a sponsor, consider committing to these visible behaviors that signal the importance of this work:

- **Model the Language**: Publicly correct destructive language when you hear it (as Jo did with Derek). Use "we" when discussing cross-functional work.
- **Protect the Rituals**: When budget pressure hits, defend collaborative rituals (joint planning, story circles, cross-functional reviews) as "critical infrastructure," not optional overhead.
- **Send Teams Back**: When conflicts are brought to you, refuse to "break the tie." Send teams back with the expectation that they return with a shared proposal.
- **Celebrate Collective Wins**: Remove functional team names from success announcements. Attribute wins only to cross-functional project names.
- **Ask the Uncomfortable Question**: In your next meeting with a peer leader, ask: "What is my team doing that makes your job harder?" Listen without defending or judgement.

Quick Wins (First 30 Days)

- Establish a 24-hour acknowledgment standard for all cross-functional inquiries
- Have each leadership team member schedule one "discovery session" with a peer (thirty minutes, no asks, only learning)
- Create a glossary of terms that mean different things to different departments
- Identify one partnership to serve as a pilot for BRIDGES-informed development or activity.

Medium-Term Initiatives (90 Days)

- Launch a "Story Circle" or equivalent ritual where achievements must be shared as collective narratives
- Implement "shadow rotations" where leaders spend time inside partner departments before big decisions
- Create at least one shared metric that requires two departments to succeed together
- Grant partner teams view-access to internal project boards ("Open Kitchen" policy)
- Conduct post-project retrospectives where individual teams cannot be named as the "cause" of failures

Structural Changes (6–12 Months)

- Abolish separate functional roadmaps; create one master document organized by business outcome
- Give partner functions veto power over new hires ("mixed interviews")
- Create budget lines that require joint signatures to unlock ("shared wallet")
- Require shadow rotations as a prerequisite for promotion to senior leadership
- Tie leadership bonuses to the same shared metrics across functions

The Seven Hidden Taxes of Organizational Silos

Every organization pays a price when its teams don't work well together, but most never realize it. The BRIDGES Model reveals seven hidden taxes, one for each stage of intergroup growth. These are not big, obvious failures. They are small, steady costs that add up over time: wasted effort, lost money, and missed chances that people write off as "just how things are."

When these taxes are left unchecked, they chip away at profits, slow down new ideas, and wear out the leaders who are supposed to be driving results. Seeing these taxes clearly is the first step toward getting rid of them.

1. The Blind Spot Tax

BRIDGES Level 1: Blocked

The Blind Spot Tax is what an organization pays when its leaders make decisions without seeing the full picture. In siloed workplaces, people regularly spend big money on products, hires, and projects using only the information their own team has.

No one checks with the group down the hall that might have the missing piece. The result is rarely one huge mistake. Instead, it is a long string of slightly off decisions that add up over time. Leaders feel confident in their choices, never knowing that the answers they needed were sitting in another department all along.

2. The Politeness Tax

BRIDGES Level 2: Receptive

The Politeness Tax is the cost of confusing good manners with real teamwork. At this stage, teams are friendly with each other. They show up to each other's meetings, share email threads, and say nice things in group settings, but the actual work still happens in separate silos.

This leads to wasted effort, with two or more teams solving the same problem without realizing it. The danger here is that everything looks fine on the surface: people are talking, calendars are full, and no one is fighting. But behind the scenes, the real work of coming together has not started, and the organization quietly pays the price.

3. The Re-Work Tax

BRIDGES Level 3: Investigating

The Re-Work Tax is the money wasted on building things that fail at launch because they were created without input from other teams.

When groups are exploring how to work together but have not yet committed to doing so, the gap between good intentions and real teamwork leads to products and plans that miss the mark.

The cost shows up as last-minute redesigns, fixes after launch, and timelines that stretch far beyond their original targets. In a factory, this looks like scrapped parts. In tech, it looks like code that has to be rewritten. In every field, it could have been avoided if teams had worked together before the build, not after the failure.

4. The Negotiation Tax

BRIDGES Level 4: Deciding

The Negotiation Tax is the time and energy teams burn when they have to fight over resources and priorities for every new project. At this level, leaders know they need to make decisions together, but they do not yet have clear rules for how to share people, money, or ownership. So every cross-team effort turns into a round of bargaining. Budget meetings get tense.

Staffing requests require backroom deals. Simple decisions stall because no one can agree on who is in charge. The real cost is not just the hours lost in meetings. It is also good ideas that never get off the ground because no one could agree on who would run them.

5. The Alignment Tax

BRIDGES Level 5: Grounded

The Alignment Tax is the ongoing cost of having to re-fight battles that should already be settled. Even in organizations where teams have found common ground, a lack of lasting agreements means that yesterday's decisions fall apart under today's pressures.

The tax shows up as the same strategy debates happening over and over, sudden changes in direction, and a growing feeling among managers that "we already decided this."

It is especially harmful to morale. Teams that worked hard to reach agreement become cynical when that agreement does not hold, and each new attempt to align feels harder than the last.

6. The Integration Tax

BRIDGES Level 6: Embedded

The Integration Tax is the huge loss of speed that happens when new teams, acquisitions, or departments try to blend into an existing organization. Even companies that are good at working across functions can stumble when the challenge grows, whether they are absorbing a competitor, adding a new division, or merging with another company.

The tax shows up as long adjustment periods, culture clashes, duplicate systems that resist being combined, and a noticeable drop in output that can last for months or even years. Organizations that have built strong internal teamwork often underestimate how much of what makes them work is unspoken, and therefore hard to pass on without focused effort.

7. The Entropy Tax

BRIDGES Level 7: Seamless

The Entropy Tax is the quiet, invisible cost of an organization slowly drifting apart. It affects even the strongest, most connected organizations, including those that have done the hard work of building seamless teamwork across groups.

Without ongoing attention, the systems, habits, and shared language that keep things running well begin to break down. Key leaders move on. Lessons learned are forgotten. Processes that once helped people stay aligned become routines that no one really understands anymore. The Entropy Tax is especially dangerous because no one notices when it is being built.

By the time the effects become clear, the organization has already slipped backward. Fighting it means treating alignment not as a finish line but as a practice, one that needs steady investment, even when everything seems to be working fine.

The Operational Glossary

The BRIDGES Model introduces a specific vocabulary to describe the invisible mechanics of trust. Use this glossary to align your team on the "new language" of high-performance connection.

Another Team

Definition: Any group, department, or division within your organization that does not report to you.

Field Note: We use this term instead of "Out-group" to remove potentially hostile framing while acknowledging the boundary.

Boundary Permeability

Definition: The ease with which information, trust, and resources flow across the line separating two teams.

Field Note: Think of this as a gate. A leader's primary job is to decide when to lock the gate (for focus) and when to open it (for speed).

Bridge Building

- **Definition**: The active behaviors a leader uses to cross organizational lines to exchange resources, information, or trust.
- **Field Note**: We use the term "Bridge Building" because it implies active construction and maintenance. "Spanning boundaries" can sound passive; building is intentional work.

The BRIDGES Model

- **Definition**: A developmental framework that maps the 7 Levels of Intergroup Leadership maturity, ranging from Blocked (Level 1) to Seamless (Level 7).

Collective Intelligence

- **Definition**: The combined problem-solving capacity of an organization.
- **Field Note**: Silos artificially lower a company's IQ by preventing the right information from reaching the right decision-maker.

The Home Team

- **Definition**: The group of people a leader identifies with, protects, and trusts implicitly (usually their direct reports).
- **Field Note**: While necessary for psychological safety, an over-reliance on the "Home Team" leads to isolation and "Fortress" behavior. (*See In-group*)

In-group

- **Definition**: In Social Identity Theory, a social group to which a person psychologically identifies as being a member.
- **Field Note**: In the BRIDGES Model, we call this The Home Team. While essential for psychological safety, unchecked in-group bias is the primary driver of silos.

Language Building Zone

- **Definition**: The asymmetric zone in the BRIDGES model which represents the amount of effort a leader requires to cultivate boundary permeability.
- **Field Note**: In this zone, a leader must "talk" their way into trust using specific, inclusive language before they can "act" their way into partnership.

Leader Language

- **Definition**: The strategic use of words, metaphors, and narratives to shape group identity and reduce hostility between teams.

- **Field Note**: We use "Leader Language" to distinguish this from formal public speaking. It is the daily "operating system" of culture, not just a speech from the stage.

Out-group

- **Definition**: In Social Identity Theory, a social group with which an individual does not identify.
- **Field Note**: In the BRIDGES Model, we call this "Another Team." Our brains are hardwired to view the out-group with suspicion, indifference, or hostility. These are the mechanisms that leaders must actively override.

The Silent Thief

- **Definition**: The invisible friction between teams that steals speed, margin, and morale without triggering a crisis alarm.
- **Field Note**: The Thief thrives in the quiet refusal to share information.

Social Identity Theory

- **Definition**: The behavioral science principle stating that humans instinctively categorize the world into "Us" (In-group) and "Them" (Out-group) to protect their self-esteem.

- **Field Note**: This is the biological root of all silos. It is not a character flaw; it is a default setting that must be actively managed.

The Story of Us

- **Definition**: A narrative technique where a leader frames success and failure as the result of the collective ecosystem, rather than specific departments.

- **Field Note**: This is the primary language tool to move from Deciding (Level 4) to Embedded (Level 6).

The 7 Levels (Archetypes)

Level 1: Blocked (The Isolated Leader)

A leader who operates a "Black Box," prioritizing the protection of their team over the needs of the organization.

Level 2: Receptive (The Aware Leader)

A leader who recognizes the friction but lacks the habits to fix it. They attend meetings but remain a "guest" in the process and participation.

Level 3: Investigating (The Open Leader)

A leader who actively maps the terrain of other departments, moving from assumption to inquiry.

Level 4: Deciding (The Connected Leader)

The tipping point where a leader consciously chooses to adopt a shared identity with another group, even when it is difficult.

Level 5: Grounded (The Aligned Leader)

A leader who has stabilized their partnerships. Communication is consistent, and the relationship can survive a crisis without blame.

Level 6: Embedded (The Collaborative Leader)

A leader who has made collaboration the default state. Teams merge workflows and co-author their future.

Level 7: Seamless (The Harmonized Leader)

The gold standard. A leader who acts as a steward, vigilantly tending the ecosystem to prevent the return of organizational silos.

Index

A

B

C

D

E

F

L

M

N

O

P

R

S

T

U

Y

About the Author

Stanton M. Brooks II is a UX veteran, product leader, and founder of Active Twist Consulting Group, LLC. With over twenty years of experience leading cross-functional teams, he developed the BRIDGES Model to give leaders the map that remains a university curriculum gap. He writes and consults at activetwist.com.

www.ingramcontent.com/pod-product-compliance
Lightning Source LLC
LaVergne TN
LVHW090512110826
845146LV00003B/828

* 9 7 9 8 9 9 5 5 2 2 4 0 9 *